Balls in a Sandwich

Balls in a Sandwich

Peter Kaye

Matador
9 Priory Business Park,
Wistow Road, Kibworth Beauchamp,
Leicestershire. LE8 0RX
Tel: 0116 279 2299
Email: books@troubador.co.uk
Web: www.troubador.co.uk/matador
Twitter: @matadorbooks

ISBN 978 1788033 640

British Library Cataloguing in Publication Data.
A catalogue record for this book is available from the British Library.

Printed and bound by CPI Group (UK) Ltd, Croydon, CR0 4YY
Typeset in 11pt Aldine401 BT by Troubador Publishing Ltd, Leicester, UK

Matador is an imprint of Troubador Publishing Ltd

Sam, Ian, Joe and Katie
and all those who give over their lives
to care for others

Bet

The last time I saw you you were in the care home. You were squashed uncomfortably into the concertinaed folds of a mechanical bed. You were only part there. You barely recognised me and were unable to converse about the strange and wonderful repetitions that ran through your mind as we used to. You said you had not had lunch - they said you had - I think you must have refused it. You were tired and sleepy but you were hungry. I stood at the top of your bed next to your soft face with sore lips. I diligently placed tiny chopped up pieces of prawn into your mouth and you obediently and hungrily accepted them. Then tiny pieces of strawberry, which you would chew uncomfortably, swallow and then gently open your mouth to receive the next miniature morsel. You were palpably uncomfortable so I followed your instructions to manoeuvre that mechanical bed into a new position. You wanted to lie back and I was very scared that you would choke in your altered position but you were very insistent. You slept. I left you.

Mary – with love

Cover illustration : Bet (2017) by Mary Trapp.
Gouache and graphite on wood (61 x 44 cm)
Copyright @ 2017 Mary Trapp
www.marytrapp.co.uk

My thanks to all my family, friends and members of the medical and support teams who have enabled me to reflect, to write and to find laughter once again.

Peter Kaye 2017

This is the day I begin to write. This is the day when I test my courage and inner strength. Part of my soul yearns to be free of the turmoil of the last couple of years; to escape the carer's so-called selfless role; to banish medical terms of 'motor neurone disease' and 'frontotemporal dementia' to the trash bin of human frailty – and to salvage what is left of my life. There has to be more than self-pity and endless blubbering tears. I have survived my first Christmas without my Bet; I have cooked Christmas lunch for what remains of my lovely family; I have forced myself to become the last minute addition to other family gatherings and, more than that, I have summoned all the brio and bravado I could muster and told everyone that I would now write a book.

I'm not sure of my motives. I'm no longer sure of anything in life – apart from the certainty that one day it will end. Writing may prove therapeutic; 'cathartic' is a good word which well-meaning friends have added to this scenario. It may, however, just condemn me to flounder even longer in this nightmare existence. It will certainly mean that I have to delve deeply into memories and these are not always the happiest of reflections. It may enable me to recapture times before dementia stole Bet – the lovely girl who had been my best friend for 56 years. It may even air brush the images of a beautiful,

1

respected body wrecked by a disease for which there is yet no effective treatment or cure.

And you the reader? How should you react? Maybe it is reassuring to know that others have faced the same uncertainties and fears that now are frightening you? Hardly comforting, I know, but sometimes it can be of help just to step off from the carer's constant treadmill – and even a brief glimpse of a life beyond can offer hope. If you are now reading this book you will know that I have survived and been able to create something tangible, and hopefully worthwhile. You may not, of course be a carer. You may have opened this book because of its title. In which case I hope you are not too disappointed!

Now I have to complete this task. There can be no excuse. I do have the title. And you must admit that it does have rather a catchy lilt.

"I want your balls in a sandwich" were the last intelligible words that Bet uttered to me. I wish I could say that they were delivered with a hint of lust – with just an intimation that our life together had been fun and fulfilled. No. It was delivered with the same degree of venom and hatred that had epitomised our last two years together. That vindictiveness that is so often a result of dementia; that acrimony that the medics will re-assure you is always directed at the one who is most loved; that constant hostility that becomes almost impossible to endure.

Survival dictates that one must search out the positives in life; that one should find humour in the darkest of situations. So please read on....

Two lives intertwined...

This book is based on my rough notes written from September 2015 when Bet finally went into permanent residential care. They were scribbled freely on train journeys or whilst waiting for my dinner to cook. I felt the need to voice my feelings and my fears. I am not sure, at that stage, that I ever considered that they would form the basis for a book.

Perhaps a brief geographical synopsis of our lives together may help you weave through my ramblings...

1943   Peter is born in Brierley, South Yorkshire
1944   Betty (Bet) is born in Fulletby, Lincolnshire
1960   They meet at The Parade Hotel, Skegness
1961   They walk together in the Pyrenees
1962   Peter begins a three year Teacher Training Course at Coventry
1963   Bet joins him at College
1965   Peter is posted by VSO to Chung Hua School, Sibu, Sarawak
1966   Bet begins teaching at Bawtry. Peter returns at Christmas
1967   Peter joins the staff at Cudworth Secondary Modern School.Bet begins teaching at Upton First School. They marry and buy a house at Thorpe Audlin

1971   Peter moves to Darfield Foulstone High as Head of English. They move to a bungalow in Hemingfield, Barnsley. Their two daughters, Rebecca and Samantha are born there.

1975   The family move to Scarborough. Peter works at The Graham School.

1984   Peter appointed Deputy Head at Launceston College in Cornwall. All the family move to Rylands on the edge of Bodmin Moor

2004   Move to Bodmin

2009   Now to Falmouth – in a flat overlooking the river

2010   A move to Arwenack Avenue where Bet has a garden once more.

2014   Move to a rented flat and then into Roscarrack Gardens…

Today she did not bite me

Wednesday 16th September 2015

The conductor on the train looks so young. He smiles, is polite and efficient. First Great Western, or Great Western Railway as it has now rebranded, employs a motley collection. I wonder if I would have been tempted if I had been fifty years younger? As a child my favourite toy had been a bus conductor's set and I know how much I wanted that captive audience. I loved going to visit Aunty Pat who lived in the next village of South Kirkby – one of the hundreds of village communities which pitted the old West Riding of Yorkshire. She lived in a house with stairs whilst Holm Lea, my home, was a bungalow. Here was my tram – my double-decker – where my passengers clung onto the hand rails and I balanced with all my three year old confidence, professionally clipping my tickets and calling out the stops. I was responsible for their journeys and all that would befall them as their lives clanked onwards.

I know how disappointed I was, many years later, when I lost the chance to fulfil this dream. A group of my friends, now looking forward to the Sixth Form at Hemsworth Grammar School, had decided to search for a holiday job. I had put forward the suggestion that we applied to work on the trams at Blackpool. My friend Gordon had a contact at The

Parade Hotel in Skegness. The toss of a coin decided our fate. Had I not gone to Skegness in the summer of 1960 I would not have knocked the tray out of Bet's hand; I would not have arrogantly made a far from charming impression and I would have never met Betty Dowse, the girl who was to become my best friend – and later my wife. Bet was now my travel companion as we laughed together at the wondrous joys we shared and comforted each other when the journey became unbearably sad. And now I am on this train, alone, pulling into Truro station on the way to see my Bet. After almost two years of caring I have given up. A nursing home now holds her broken body and distorted mind – and I feel as though I have let her down. I have failed. My heart feels broken. The tears are again in my eyes.

I leave the station, cross over a footbridge and walk down through a pleasant estate of private houses. The roadway crosses a small stream and I begin the very steep climb up Comprigney Hill towards Kenwyn. This is my personal exercise. It is my way of refusing to acknowledge that prostate cancer could ever defeat me. It is my way of sticking two fingers up at my more recent diagnosis of Diabetes Type 2. I have given up the cakes and biscuits, lost 8lbs in five weeks and I am beginning to wish that I hadn't invested in 38 inch waisted trousers. One of the problems of having an M&S store nearby is that it's far too easy to 'click and collect' with that button! Thankfully daughter Sam did persuade me not to donate my entire 36 inch collection to charity shops. Ever grateful my lovely! Sam is an absolute treasure. Having lost her elder sister eight years ago (Becca died of metastatic melanoma in 2007) she now found her mother was 'away with the fairies' (albeit in a wheelchair) and her father has cancer.

Bet is in bed when I arrive. She claims she has had no lunch – but she probably refused to have any when, no doubt, it was offered. Her food has to be pureed now as she can no longer swallow anything solid and although arranged logically on a plate with scoops of relevant colours – it never looks too appetising. I open the cool bag that I have carried fastidiously from home. Inside are some tiny bite size sandwiches, made as moist as I can with thick beef (!) pate and loads of butter. One by one Bet is able to suck them and they slide down her throat. I now feed her the crushed peach which has been kept cool and she enjoys. She no longer feeds herself. She has had no use of her left arm and hand for many months and now there is very limited ability in her right hand. Left to her own devises she would still attempt to eat independently and would force food into her mouth. The resulting choking fit would be distressing; the mess created would be reminiscent of a demented toddler discovering chocolate mouse. So I now take my time, ensuring that each mouthful is swallowed before the next is offered. I tend now to use a spoon – although it is several weeks since she last attempted to bite my finger.

I can't remember exactly when the aggression surfaced. It was two years ago that we began to piece together the fragments of strange behaviour. Christmas 2013 was bizarre and frightening. I came home one day from a voluntary shift in The Poly Box Office to find the hallway cluttered with carrier bags stuffed full with towels and tea towels. These were for Sam, Bet insisted. Sam wanted them. A few hours later and Bet was boiling up a soup, throwing in herbs and spices with a strange abandonment – even though we had eaten (yet another heavily spiced creation into which every available herb had been flung!). This was for our friend Ian B, claimed Bet. His partner Sue had died and he was coming over to be fed. I was now in a strange new world. I tried to reason but Bet was adamant. She was right and I was wrong. I argued. I became frustrated and angry. I now know, of course, that my reaction would only have caused Bet more anxiety. Dementia requires one to enter into the "new" world and accept it. It is pointless and counter productive to challenge. But then I knew little about dementia – and certainly nothing about how the carer should react. A battle ground of arguments and tears ensued. This was not how our lives should be. We had never fought like this. I know she made it clear that she now hated me – but I am not sure at what stage she first hit me.

I do know that as 2014 progressed I had learned that avoidance tactics were my best protection. There would be finger nails digging deep into my arm and kicks as I passed by. But it was after we moved into Roscarrack Gardens late in the year that physical violence reached its disturbing peak. She hated the bungalow and the fact that it had been purposely designed for wheelchair use. It also had a very useful wet room which made it easier for me to manage her daily shower. Initially she could walk in with my help. I would take my clothes off too and wash myself down at the same time. Not a good idea – for Bet would always give me a whacking thump in the testicles. Initially it would make me cry. This was not the physical hurt so much but the fact that she wanted to boost up the prostate cancer cells and speed up my demise. "They only hurt the ones they love" was of little consolation!

Early in 2015 Chris, our very helpful physiotherapist, was to sneak in a shower stool. Bet was still in total denial that anything was really wrong with her – and was strident in her refusal to accept help. But when once the stool was in place it was accepted. A tremendous help to us both – but now she was seated the kicks too could be aimed into my groin. My friend Pat, from school days, tells me that she almost sent me a cricket box for my birthday. Thankfully I remained quite agile – if occasionally bruised. Avoiding being bitten was a further bathroom sport. Bet would swiftly strike at my shoulder as I dried her hair. I did shock a few visitors as I revealed the teeth marks – the trophies of my life now. I needed to share this with others. At this stage I was still dealing with this alone. Help was always there in the wings – but Bet's condition dictated that this could not be deployed. One may ask why I continued to battle without help. I am no longer sure why. I know that she felt that she was well – or that was what she consistently asserted. There was a slight physical problem, she admitted, but that could easily be remedied if I could find her the right chiropractor. She was angry and distressed if I should suggest any other form of help. If I loved her, she would claim, I would not need others to help. And I did love her.

Throughout this last year she has continued to physically abuse others who came too close. It seems that with Frontotemporal Dementia (FTD) the personality completely changes. The caring person now lacks empathy; kisses become bites; hugs become thumps; and love becomes hate. When Sue (the one who had died) came to visit, Bet gave her quite a striking bite on her cheek. Not quite hard enough to draw blood but enough to shock. The next day I talked to Bet about the incident. Bet had lost her easy and beautiful ability to smile but it was obvious from the contortions of her mouth that she was looking back with a degree of pleasure. It was Sue's partner Ian B, of course, that Bet believed would one day come and carry her off to some romantic dalliance. In the very early stages of this nightmare we had joined friends, including Sue and Ian B, at a meal in a local Thai Restaurant. Bet had purposefully seated herself next to Ian B and throughout the evening she had caressed his leg! Thankfully we have very understanding friends – and yes, I still loved her.

When I didn't cry, I would laugh. A sort of nervous laugh which reminded me of when I was a little boy.

My dad was a miner. A shift worker. There would be times when it was wise to be quiet but I couldn't always gauge it correctly. I could see my dad's anger rising, his face getting redder and his eyes watering. I knew how this would end. It always ended in the same way. I would laugh nervously, a reaction, like blinking, that I couldn't avoid. I was told to wipe the grin off my face – but the pathway was already set. The inevitable hard smack would follow, sometimes so hard that it would knock me to the ground. Not that I look back on my dad with any hatred or anger. He was a good man. He was clever too. Quite a brilliant mathematician I remember. As a child he had won a scholarship to the local grammar school but his parents wouldn't allow him to go. He was the eldest of three children and expected to work as soon as he was able.

He had tried hard to escape the mine – the inevitable and cruel fate of generation after generation of the Kaye's. I remember how my mother fondly told of their 'courting days' when 'Bert would meet Grace as she flaunted her long strands of auburn hair on the swings at Brierley Park. He would bring her biscuits from the Coop where he proudly worked. Sadly the colliery would pay him more money. He had no choice. The lure of the mine. I was asked fairly recently why miners kept pigeons. I couldn't give an answer there and then, but the question stayed with me and I later wrote a poem:

The little boy, skinny legged and tousled hair
Kicked at the shimmering gorse
Hid from the silver birch guards
And rescued the sun beams on his phantom horse
High above the skylark sang full throttled
And gloriously clear
All was so well with this world
There was nothing at all to fear.

But the sky lark saw what the boy did not
As her eyes scanned the valley below
The coal mines belched forth a blackness
A wasteland that would grow and grow
Here on the sandy ridge the boy froze
A lone miner stood – as though at journey's end
Strong, silent, sinewed – staring
Into the valley – reluctant to descend

Lark, boy and man – suddenly caught in awe
The flurry of pigeons, circling, caressing the sun
For a brief moment resting on the summer air
Their race was almost won.
Then they were gone – plunged deep
Towards the lofts – like prison bars below
The corn tin rattled – the trap was set
The valley calls and all must go.

The miner looked up
His tired eyes rimmed with the blackness of toil
He began his walk downward
Each step dragging at innocent soil

Before him the pit head
The winding gear – the open cage
The rattle of the coal dust
The lure of a wage.

The boy and the lark played on

Peter Kaye 2012

The little boy was me of course, carefree amongst the bracken and birch trees of Brierley Common – a beautiful open space high above the valleys steaming and choking with the fumes of the pits and coke ovens. Of course the mines are no longer and the valleys are healthier places. Bet and I later returned to South Yorkshire and listened to the ghosts whispering – echoes of the hundreds of poor souls who gave their lives in the interests of progress. When I researched my family history I came to realise the sheer cruelty of our search for coal. I drew a ten mile radius around my birth place, listed all the collieries and researched the mining disasters. The result was another poem:

Monkton,
Fitzwilliam, Askern
Monk Bretton, (where my Granny Kettles★ was born – and
    my dad)
Brierley (where I was born and grew up)
Brodsworth, Hickleton Main (my dad worked there)
Thurcroft, Tinsley Park
South Kirkby (where my Mum was born – and her dad)

(Her dad worked there too.)
The Oaks at Barnsley (360 men and boys killed there in
     1866)
Barnsley – hit again – 143 died at Swaith Main in 1875
Crofton, Denaby in 1912 – 88 lost their lives
Wharnecliffe – 58 died in 1936
Markham, two years later, and 79 blown to bits
Such is the toll in these Yorkshire pits.

Kilnhurst, Herringthorpe, Thrybergh Hall
Manvers, Maltby, Wombwell, Wath
Grimethorpe, Ferrymoor (my Granddad Kettles worked
     there)
Dinnington, Marton
Firbeck, Barley Hall
Cadeby – all hold their ghosts.
Men swallowed whole
Lives lost in search of coal.

Edlington, Corton Wood
Barnborough, Conisborough (where my other granny was
     born)
Rockingham, Silkstone
Elsecar and Aldwarke Main
Woolley (where granddad was born – that's Granddad
     Kettles)
His dad died aged 21.
Ten years in the pits and he was done.

Silverwood, Frickley, Houghton Main
Gawber Goldthorpe, Shireoaks, Birley East,

Lundhill – another place to echo
This time with 189 human cries
Listen now to the silent sighs.

Where were the voices of protest?
As men spent their lifetime in night
Far too easy to ignore this torture
Far too easy to switch on the light

Peter Kaye 2012

* *Granny 'Kettles' is really Granny Kaye – my father's mother. She had a collection of miniature brass kettles on her sideboard – hence her name!*

That perhaps explains why I get so rattled when local people moan about wind farms or object to solar panels. My dad was to spend most of his life 'down the pit' and he did keep pigeons. He also played snooker very successfully spending much of his free time at The 'Stute – The Village Institute. As a very small boy I would sometimes go with him until I came home one evening and stated that I didn't want any 'bloody' rice pudding! That was the end of that! Mother would not allow me there again for a very long time.

My mother did go to the Grammar School and made the most of it. She was born in March 1914 in South Kirkby. Her father Bill, a miner, was soon to join up into the army at the beginning of The First World War. My granddad carried shrapnel in his shoulder for the rest of his life and never spoke of the horrors he had endured. His younger brother Herbert was killed on the first day of the Battle of the Somme – and from that point onwards granddad rejected the strict faith of his childhood. Her mother Florence took Grace, her only child, initially to live with Grandie Simpson in Moorthorpe but by the time my mum won her scholarship to Hemsworth Grammar School in 1923 she had lived in nine different homes and had attended five different schools. My mum was to thoroughly enjoy her time at Hemsworth and particularly relished acting. She took up a post as an unqualified teacher at Common Road Infant School, South Kirkby, where the Headmistress persuaded her to apply to the West Riding Teacher Training College at Bingley. In the summer of 1937 Grace became a fully qualified teacher – and the trend began. The genetic chain was broken and I would be free from the shackles of the mines.

When I later came to read "Sons and Lovers" by D H Lawrence I thought of my own parents as being similar to Gertrude and Walter Morel. My mother was obviously the driving force and had ambitions. Her son would never have to go down the mines. For as long as I could remember it was expected that I would pass the 11+ and would enjoy literature. We had a set of encyclopaedias full of pictures of Greek statues and famous buildings – and these were brought out whenever friends from the village came to play. As many of the statues were naked figures I think it gained me some degree of popularity. When I did go to the grammar school then I found myself following my mother's love of the stage. I was in every annual production, winning the Dramatic Arts Cup two years in succession. Mother was pleased.

My dad struggled to bond with me. I remember how disappointed he had been, when he had taken me, at the age of five, to Oakwell to watch Barnsley play football. Apparently I read a comic throughout the match. He wanted me to share his love of snooker – but mother had squashed that on the grounds that it taught me filthy language. She was right, of course, for the "Stute" was an all male preserve inhabited by miners. There was a code. Pit language was never to be used in front of the women or children. It was years before I fully appreciated the intricacies of 'pit language'. Once every month as the teacher in charge of 'careers' at Cudworth Secondary Modern School I took a dozen lads down Grimethorpe Colliery. I could not believe, nor calculate, the number of times the word 'fucking' could be woven into a sentence. How times have changed.

It was to be many years later that I was to feel close to my father. Whilst teaching in Scarborough I had developed an interest in timetable construction. Way before computers were to deprive creative teachers of creativity this was a mathematical challenge. At the Graham School it was exciting – intoxicating – mind blowing. Imagine five days of school time divided into twenty minute modules. Seventy teachers and sixty five rooms on three sites miles apart. All to be constructed on giant peg boards which took up a whole room. Forget the fact that site 'three' was the

Sea Training Wing and dependent on tides – the rest was a synch. 409,500 pegs (135 different colours and symbols) all to be slotted into place to make a coherent working pattern for 1600 pupils. The Head, when I had moved to Scarborough in 1975, was Miss Briggs. In the first years of this newly created comprehensive school Miss Briggs had insisted on constructing the timetable for Year One (now called Year 7) herself – from scratch with a completely empty board. When satisfied she would then hand over the task to her Faculty Heads who would struggle to complete the puzzle without daring to touch the boss's work. The story goes that one year a cleaner allowed the door to slam and Miss Brigg's labours tumbled over the floor. The cleaner was horrified and placed the pegs back – making patterns of colour. It turned out to be the best timetable Hilda Briggs ever created. How I remember working in that claustrophobic environment night after night. A school at midnight is an eerie place. Bet never complained. She would always support and understand me – always be there when I got home no matter what the time.

Little wonder then that I wanted to design a more family friendly way to construct the timetable. I turned to paper and pencil – and to my father. In 1982 I talked to him about the challenges and he was animated. His interest in mathematics had not left him and he wanted to help. How tragic that he died later that year. We could have made a great team.

Bet has now closed her eyes. No violence today. No harsh words. I know she sometimes lashes out at the carers here. They assure me that they are used to this and don't take it to heart. They don't know my Bet though! They only know this twisted body and this tortured soul.

I leave for my walk back down the hill to the station. Today I can smile. Today she did not bite me.

"I love you Maggie!"

Friday 18ᵗʰ September 2015

I drive into Truro today – collecting Maggie en route. We have lunch on the way and I enjoy having the company. It is now so comforting to have someone with me as we walk down the long corridor, past the dining room and through the freshly decorated coffee lounge. Maggie seems well impressed. Bet's room is in a newly refurbished wing. There are no 'care home' smells; no heavily stained carpets and the atmosphere is more like a five star hotel. This is why Sam and I had chosen to place Bet in Kenwyn. Not that there was much choice. Most nursing homes we had visited had no immediate vacancies – and most were drably furnished, dark and unwelcoming. Bet had fought constantly against going into care and it was the hardest decision I have ever had to make.

Everyone, the medical team who supported me, Sam and Ian, my friends, had all agreed that this was the only possible decision. It was obviously very hard for me to admit that I could no longer cope and that there may be others better able to deal with Bet's complex needs – even though we now had a brilliant team of carers who popped in to help. The little bungalow was heaving with equipment on loan to us. Bet had a hospital style bed which she hated; she had a commode which she abhorred; there were two hoists which proved impossible for me to handle especially as Bet would physically fight to escape any form of stricture. I had bought a wheel chair which she would occasionally and very begrudgingly use. We also had bought a high rise chair but Bet constantly found fault with that. It's high arms caused her to spill her tea and its uncomfortable cushions were responsible for her 'uncontrolled leg jerks' – the kicks which occurred whenever I passed by. She hated everything. Me especially – and the house was not far behind.

We had moved to Falmouth in May 2009. We wanted to be near the sea again and our years in Bodmin had been full of sadness. We had reluctantly moved to the old county town in 2004, leaving our beloved 'Rylands' just outside the village of Altarnun on the eastern edge of Bodmin Moor. Mother had decided that we should live in Bodmin – it was not our first choice but it enabled mum to keep her doctor – and apparently at the age of 91 that is important. We had chosen quite a modern house which had a lovely couple of rooms which mum could call her own. Mum had needed care and that was then to become our priority. There was never any doubt that we would look after her. Bet was just so calm and loving. She always had been and I assumed that she always would surround us all with love. For the next six months one or the other of us would always be there for Mum. Bet and I would take turns to visit Sam, Ian and now little Joe in Bristol. It was on one such journey, when I had just arrived at Sam's house, that I got the call from Bet to tell me that Mum had collapsed and had been rushed into hospital. A quick sandwich and I was back on the M5. Mum had had a stroke and was never to properly recover.

There were to be several weeks in the local hospital where Mum's behaviour became more and more bizarre. I suppose this was my first real experience of dementia – and it was the sort that was funny – at least for some people. Mum decided that she would run a radio broadcasting system from her hospital bed. She would blare out the adverts in what I called her 'telephone voice' – drawing on her histrionic youth – as "Aaarsda paastar" and other special offers were reverberated around the ward at ever more frequent intervals. I have a vivid memory of Bet and I visiting Mum one morning. By the first bed, physically shaking and looking desperately tired, was a dear frail old lady in tears .

"It's your mother", she blubbered, "She's been broadcasting all night!"

Later that day mum was moved into an individual side ward. Unfortunately it had a mirrored wardrobe at the foot of the bed. Mother could now see herself. Her television station now began to broadcast! The histrionics were even more flamboyant. Within days we were asked to move mum into a nursing home. We found a place in Launceston and Mum was transported there by ambulance on a Monday evening. Our daughter Becca lived in the town and visited her granny who had seemed rather distressed. Bet and I went over the moor early the next day – only to find that Mum had died during the night. She had suffered a perforation of the colon. She should not have been moved. I hoped that she had not suffered pain – but I suspect she died in agony.

Bet and I realised that for the first time for many years we were free to concentrate on ourselves. Little did we know, in those brief halcyon few days, that our beautiful world was about to be shattered. But it was – and for the next two years we were to surrender our entire existence to supporting our elder daughter Becca and her devoted partner Kev as she bravely fought against the encroaching ravages of metastatic melanoma. And so our house in Bodmin continued its role as a base for our shattered bodies and minds – and after Becca died we needed to move.

And why Falmouth? It had been Becca's suggestion. During her terminal illness we had encouraged her and Kev to 'take off' and do whatever they thought that they would like to do. They went off to stay in a remote light house on the North Devon coast; they hired an old boat house on the edge of the sea at Coverack; and they stayed in a bothy near the Glendurgan Estate. From here they had visited Falmouth and on their return Becca had told us that it was our 'kind of place' and that I would 'love it'. After Becca's death, Bet and I came down to the town. Our daughter knew us so well. It was 'our kind of place' – the sea, the ferries, the coastal walks, the Natural Health shop, the Poly Arts Centre – and even a Marks and Spencers!

We moved into a flat with a wonderful view over the river to Flushing. I was captivated by that view and

Bet realised that. She embraced my enthusiasm at the time – but I later realised that she was compromising on her own desire to have a garden. I should have realised and I have beaten myself mentally many times since. It is not, I tell myself, that I have always made the decision as to where we should live. When we moved homes in Scarborough, to a house with a sea view and a fourth bedroom (so we could look after my grandmother) Bet viewed the house alone. We bought it without me ever seeing inside. Our friend Fran tells me that Bet and I had a relationship of equal halves and I have found that to be so reassuring – a great relief over the past couple of years.

Without a garden our new home may have been – but typically Bet threw herself fully into our latest life in this different community. In days we hade made 'friends' within our block. This had always been our approach to life. Bet would smile at everyone – and expected a smile in return. A simple ambition in life but one that usually worked. We invited neighbours round for supper and our hospitality was appreciated and usually returned. We helped collect shopping and Bet cooked meals for Mrs B when she broke her wrist. We introduced ourselves to Sue and Ian B when they arrived back from Europe in their motor home – even though we had been warned not to get involved as Sue 'could be trouble'. That was a side of this new community that disturbed us. We had no intention of avoiding anyone but it was a decision that was to cause us much grief a few months later. Sue could be 'trouble' but for reasons that were just and sound. Sue knew when things were wrong and unfair and she was not afraid to stand up against any oppressor. She was a Yorkshire lass!

What was the source of this 'trouble? Car parking! What else! In this world where half the population is starving and where thousands of families risk their lives to find freedom – what do the good folk of this community find so critical? So called appointed 'directors' had decided that it was beneficial to charge flat owners for parking in the communal parking areas and thereby reducing the annual community charge. We got embroiled – or at least I did. We thought the policy unfair and when friends Joan and Peter were threatened with court action we felt we should offer them support. We had a good friend Robert back in Scarborough. Retired now, but he had been a solicitor for his working life and knew his way round the complexities and vagaries of flat leases. I asked his opinion and he agreed that the directors were wrong. Sadly the 'directors' did not agree – and so began a battle which was to last for a year. Immediately Bet and I tried to conciliate we found that the 'directors' and many more of our new 'friends' no longer spoke to us. The camp was divided. We too were now classed as 'trouble makers'. Bet was stunned by this behaviour. Mrs B told her that she would never speak to her again; fellow neighbours would turn away rather than meet in the street. Bet was heart broken. She could never understand how people could behave in this way. We had lost our daughter. Surely there were more important things in life than cars and parking them?

How could people place material things above love, tolerance and compassion? It did mean, however, that we put the flat on the market. Bet would have her garden again. It also meant that the 'trouble makers' became a closer group of friends – especially as by the end of the year our case had been won. Maggie was a stalwart part of this group. Bet and I were so pleased to be counted as a friend of Maggie – for she would have made a formidable enemy.

Maggie has a replacement knee, with a metal socket that creaks when she walks. She has had her hip replaced twice – the last time with a metal rod that is two inches too short. There is a metal plate in there too. The last time Maggie flew anywhere was in 2010 when she went up to Durham to visit her son. The alarms were set off as she went through the security barriers and she was swiftly isolated. She has survived at least three heart attacks and nine months after having a stent fitted she had a triple by pass operation. Three weeks later she suffered a heart attack and was glad that she was still in 'intensive care'. Maggie stopped counting her age five years ago when she was 80!

And now Maggie is close to me as we turn into Bet's room. I never know what I will find. I am sure my anxiety is palpable. Today Bet is sitting in her arm chair near the window. The television is on but Bet's face immediately turns towards us. For the last two years I have found it impossible to predict any reaction so there is considerable relief when it becomes obvious that Bet is pleased to see Maggie. Her smile, once so easy and engaging, is now just about recognisable but the effort is so unmistakable. Her speech is also beginning to suffer. There is just a hint of slurring, an indication of the rapid decline of Bet's ability to communicate which is now to set in with an alarming vengeance. Bet asks a few questions. They are short and direct but are relevant. Bet's capacity to understand the situation is still pertinent. Some issues are fully understood; others seem impossible for Bet to grasp. Just for now I am grateful, for Maggie's sake, that Bet seems aware and responsive. There follows the usual ritual of opening the cool box and revealing the little tubs of special treats. Today I have brought a prawn cocktail followed by strawberries and cream, Again Bet enjoys them. Slow progress but I am contented. It is a good thing to do especially as Bet is now eating so little. We clean Bet's teeth. I would worry that the care staff seemed to neglect her lovely teeth – but I have come to realise that she is refusing to allow them near her mouth. This was to be part of our daily tasks – our shared time together.

Bet then looks straight at Maggie. There is an intensity in her eyes that I had witnessed on many occasions. I hoped that venom was not about to pour forth.

"I love you Maggie," she clearly enunciates.

Tears come into Maggie's eyes – and then into mine. What a lovely moment and one that Maggie will never forget.

This wasn't the first time that Maggie and I had shared tears and I don't suppose it will be the last.

Maggie has had more than her fair share of sorrow. Her father and brother were lost at sea. In 1941 her father was commanding the 'Kyle Roma' as she carried coal from Portreath to Maryport. Her brother Kenneth, at the very last minute, had taken the place of a seaman who was ill. He didn't normally sail with his father. The boat disappeared and the two men were never seen again. When the sun went down they were part of a convoy and as the sun rose they were gone. What happened has remained a mystery. Never a scrap of debris was ever found, casting doubts on the most likely theory that the boat had been torpedoed. Maggie's mother was left with five children to look after and no income. It took her a whole year, tribunal after tribunal, to get the admiralty to accept that the boat had been lost through enemy action and not negligence by Maggie's father. Maggie still has tears in her eyes whenever she relates these memories. We share tears too when Maggie talks about her brother Frederick.

Frederick, like his father and brother Kenneth, was seven feet tall and exceptionally good looking. As a youngster he had fallen down stairs and as a result suffered damage to his bones and muscles. For the rest of his life he would have to wear a calliper and special boot; he would shake violently when under stress as the bones pressed onto his nerves: he would easily lose balance and fall and his head could not be supported leading him to become bent. He grew into a gentle young man however and was obviously intelligent. Maggie fondly tells the story of how he helped his friend, who had won a place at the local Grammar School, complete his homework – even though Frederick had been unable to go into senior school as it was too far away for him to walk. He never could hold down a 'proper' job but became a skilled craftsman taking great pride in his carpentry. Sadly he died at the age of 29. I mention this because it perhaps explains why Bet and I found Maggie to be a kindred spirit. We had known sadness and loss; we had known family members who had struggled to be accepted in their lives.

My sister Pauline was born in 1947 when I was three years old. There was a problem at her birth and the umbilical cord, wrapped round her throat, had deprived her brain of oxygen. It became obvious months later that Pauline would have problems throughout her life. She was classed as 'spastic' – that term which thankfully has now been banished from most people's vocabulary. She would eventually walk – but always with an ungainly gait; she would never be able to understand mathematics; but, thanks to Mum's patience Pauline was to develop a fine vocabulary and a skill at spelling that I couldn't match until I became an English Teacher and had to sort myself out! Pauline was to suffer from epilepsy and until it became controlled by medication there were bouts of physical violence and anti-social patterns of behaviour. As the elder brother I was expected to shoulder much responsibility for her care – and I have been reminded of that experience a great deal over the past two years. Pauline was tremendously sociable and would talk to any one. Conversation was not always appropriate and I still remember acute embarrassment at my sister's behaviour. Dad found this particularly difficult to deal with. At that time there was still a feeling that to have a 'handicapped child' was a reflection on the family. People were still 'put away' into mental institutions and 'care in the community' was a topic never mentioned. It did exist however – and probably more so than today. For families rallied round and the nucleus of care was still evident. Now I was reminded of those days.

Pauline had once wandered alone into the large forest which bounded our grandfather's garden. There was a large lake in these woods and there was great concern for her safely. A bevy of the local police force arrived and after several hours of searching there was a tearful reunion. At least my mother was tearful. Pauline was oblivious to the concern. She had followed a butterfly into the woods, had become lost and had eventually fallen asleep in the sunshine. There the friendly arms of our local copper had scooped her up and delivered her home. Now Bet had behaved in the same way. At times she would fail to meet up with me at agreed places in town. I would call into the shops where she had been. She had been there, she was always remembered, but now where had she gone? I would dash home now becoming concerned for her safety. Then I would get a puzzled phone call from a friend to say that Bet was with them. Did I know? Bet seemed uncertain about where she was supposed to be. She was oblivious to the worry she had caused me. Initially these episodes were annoying but they were to become more frequent and potentially dangerous.

Pauline also, despite her apparent frailty, could lash out violently. I can still clearly see her picking up a clock from the mantelpiece and hurling it towards me. I can still sense the nervous grin as my father blamed me for the incident. Another whack! Now over sixty years later I am dealing with Bet's nails digging into my flesh and the nervous laugh returns. Pauline's behaviour was not always aggressive. She loved people and was hugely gregarious. With the naivety and innocence that can sometimes make those with mental problems so adorable she would talk to anyone and everyone. Free from the shackles of social conventions, Bet was now the same. Whenever we were out walking she would speak to everyone we met. She had always been hugely sociable but now it was obsessional. However, she no longer had the open smile that had always been the charm. It was obvious to all who met her that she had 'some kind of problem'. Of course she was now either clinging to my arm for support or in her wheelchair. Not everyone knows how to deal with such situations – in fact surprisingly few people are at ease. I still noticed that people we knew would cross over to the other side of the road rather than talk to us. A sad reflection on 'care in the community' and the 'dementia friendly' signs that are now appearing in shop windows. We still have a long way to go.

Maggie had no such problems and continued to

treat Bet with dignity and respect whenever they met. Bet hated to be patronised and even in her darkest moments she was acutely aware when friends didn't talk to her as they previously would have done. I was so often guilty myself of treating her abruptly and I hated myself. Too easy to speak without thinking – to retaliate when I could no longer understand how she was behaving nor make sense of her reactions. No wonder she hated me so often. I so frequently failed to understand her world and she could not understand my frustrations, anger and tears. I am sure that she manipulated me with the way she would juxtaposition love and hate. I would sometimes still try to introduce logic into perplexing situations. I would find myself explaining that as she no longer loved me then perhaps it would be better if I found her somewhere else to live. Not a good idea. There was so much anger at the thought that I would place her in care. I tried other tactics. As she hated me then why should I cook her supper? If there was the slightest suggestion that she may be deprived of food then she would claim to love me – although as soon as the food was prepared it would be back to hate. But now , this afternoon, it was clear that she loved Maggie – and there had been no hatred shown to me.

Before we leave I mention that I may go and see Peter and Joan. They now lived on the Isle of Wight – having left the flats soon after we had escaped. It is not easy to tell Bet that I would not be visiting her for a few days – and I think I only dare mention this because Maggie is with me and the mood is relaxed.

32

Maggie helps. She asks Bet what I should bring her back as a present. A pebble from the beach. A simple pebble. That's all she wants.

We leave smiling. I love you too Maggie!

"I need a chiropractor! Get me a bloody chiropractor!"

Thursday 24th September 2015

On the train again – and my fourth hike up Comprigney Hill this week. The pounds are falling off me – and the bulging tummy, which Bet found so disgusting, is beginning to disappear. I will point this out to her, of course, but I doubt she will show any interest. She certainly won't bless me with any credit.

As I walk past the dining room I see Bet in there, hunched in her wheelchair. One of the male carers, let's call him Ken, is just about to feed her, so I take over. He has remembered that she likes garlic mushrooms and he has brought her a bowl full. They slip down easily and she loves the flavour. Her own cooking had always used herbs and spices and we had used organic vegetables wherever possible. During the past two years her appetite has changed dramatically – and now has almost diminished completely. Garlic mushrooms remain the one dish on the house menu that she seems to enjoy. I have my cool bag with me and I know she will seem to relish today's little pots of fruits.

Ken pops over to ask if everything is fine.

"How much do you earn?" Bet asks him directly and with a strange urgency.

"Not enough!" he responds with a grin. He walks on down the corridor ever alert to the constant call bells and flashing lights that dominate the carer's life.

"Follow him!" Bet shouts at me. "Follow him to his room. We need to talk to him!"

I begin to push Bet along the corridor towards her own room but she is agitated and seems distressed.

"Not my room – his!" She is now yelling at me and is obviously angry. "We can pay him more than he earns now. He can come to our house and look after me there! We need to sort this out. I need to come home!"

There is some logic in her argument. I can feel the guilt rising within me. The tears are welling up in my eyes. I do the usual and try to placate and distract. I place Bet by the window and ask if she has seen the squirrel this morning for he often plays on the lawns. I open the cool bag and offer her some apricot mixed with peach, followed by a yoghurt. I then give her one of the cherry liquor chocolates that I keep in one of the drawers. I clean her teeth and wash out her mouth with the mouth-wash that she likes – all a bit messy after chocolate but now an established part of our routine. I rub her legs and arms with 'Hippy Rose Body Lotion' which has been a favourite for quite a few years.

"I need a chiropractor! Get me a bloody chiropractor!"

How many times have I tried to answer this? I used to try to clarify how we had been to several chiropractors, that each one had tried to help, but they had all explained that there were problems which they couldn't cure. I now simply told her that we were still searching – and that somewhere there would be a chiropractor who did have a magic wand.

"I can come home now, can't I?"

"I'm sorry my love. I can't look after you by myself can I? And our little house isn't big enough for Ken to live there too. He has his own family to look after doesn't he?" I cannot begin to count the number of times I have struggled to talk through my tears.

Bet is silent. Has she accepted that it is impossible for her to return home or is she bitterly disappointed, sick with contempt, at my patronising response? I can never know.

"Shall I read to you now?" I ask.

She nods and I pick up the latest book I am reading to her. It is "The Amazing Story of Adolphus Tips" by Michael Morpurgo. My granddaughter Katie has loaned it to us.

Katie is nine years old – but has a wisdom far beyond her years. She has shown a remarkable understanding of the sadness I feel and has an impressive and oh so welcome ability to make me laugh. In July, after Bet had gone into a care home for two weeks in order to give me a respite break, Sam had arranged for me to take Katie to Heligan Gardens. There Kneehigh Theatre were presenting "943" – an adaptation of "Adolphus Tips" – and Sam had got us tickets for the matinee. As we set off Katie had commented on my attire.

"Don't you ever wear anything else?" she asked.

I was in my shorts as usual – but I did point out that I frequently changed them – and that my T shirt was clean. Katie was in rain gear and well prepared. I had failed to notice that this was a typical July day with Cornish mizzle and a cold wind blowing. I did need a break!

"To stop you feeling lonely today I am going to pretend to be Bet Bet!" she laughed.

And then she punched my arm! "Perhaps not!" she added with her wide grin.

It proved to be a lovely day. My grandchildren are such good company. I remember a visiting District Nurse reminding me that I had a life beyond looking after Bet.

"Remember that you are a father – and also a grandfather", she said. That simple statement has meant so much to me.

Bet now wants the television back on. The programme seems irrelevant. The tea trolley comes round and I indulge in a piece of chocolate cake! Bet now wants the blessed commode so I ring the call bell and prepare to leave. I don't like to see her being transported via a hoist. It looks so uncomfortable and I know how she resents not being able to move by herself. I try to convince myself that she will be happier if I leave. It may be, of course, that she was.

I leave for the train reminding her that tomorrow Mary will be calling to see her and that I have left fruit and yoghurt in the fridge. I tell her again that Sam and the children will be in to see her on Saturday and Sunday and that Sue and Ian will be in on Monday and Ann and Kevin on the Tuesday. I will travel back from the Isle of Wight on Tuesday and be in as usual on Wednesday. She seems to understand – and the list of visitors is reassuring. She likes people to visit. Not every one likes to visit Bet however, a source of much distress to me over the past months.

The walk down to the station helps to clear my thoughts. It is good that I am going away for a few days. And Joan and Peter are such welcome company. After the 'agitators' had won our battle over car park charges we had found ourselves in 'The Boathouse' – drinking to our success. It seemed a hollow triumph – a victory in a battle which should never have been fought. It was February 2011 and Sue and Ian B were about to set off in their motor home into Europe – probably Portugal. I think it was my idea that the rest of us should fly out and join Sue for her birthday in March. I did tend to come up with wild suggestions – something Bet had accepted (dare I suggest loved?) in our life together. During the past two years she has constantly told me that I am no longer the amusing, lovely person that she married. I used to make her laugh – but no longer. She seems to hold me entirely responsible for the fact that our life together is now so different.

Sue and Ian B left for the continent a few days after our conquest over the penny pinching, bean counting antics of our neighbours. I began to look at flights to Lisbon or Faro. They seemed pleasantly affordable and Bet and I were looking forward to another 'expedition' for it seemed a long while since we had been on a holiday. In 2007, just after Becca had died, we had escaped into the Alps of Austria and walked furiously as some form of therapy. Now it would be different. We would try to relax. Sue, however, kept emailing from their latest camp site. She seemed uncertain as to where they would be by the time of her birthday. Every day the cost of the air tickets was rising and the thought of relaxation was evaporating rapidly. Then Joan took matters in hand. The bomb shell exploded.

"We are all going on a cruise!" she announced. The shockwaves echoed to the tune of her strident Glaswegian accent. Bet and I were stunned.

Now a 'cruise' was never something Bet and I had considered. In fact it could be said that it was, to us, an anathema – something totally out of our comfort zone.

"We don't do cruises!" Bet stated rather disparagingly. "I haven't got a frock!"

This was a slight exaggeration for Bet, who was certainly happiest in her denims, had at least one dress which she saved for special occasions.

"That's fine," Joan volleyed back. "This isn't that type of cruise. This is informal. You can wear whatever you like."

"We enjoy walking," Bet retaliated. This was beginning to resemble the Battle of Culloden. "I can think of nothing worse that sitting on a ship in the middle of the ocean!"

"Exactly!" came the agreement. "This cruise will drop us off every morning at a different port on a different island – and we can all enjoy our walks together."

Within the hour all four of us were in the travel agents at the bottom of High Street, flashing our passports and signing our cheques. In three weeks we were boarding our boat in Madeira en route, via Agadir, for the Canary Islands. It was March and the sea could get a bit rough – but we thoroughly enjoyed the experience – the food, the cocktails, the walks, the friendliness of the multi cultural crew and above all the company of Joan and Peter.

Sadly the experience was later to play heavily on Bet's mind. In Agadir walking was not recommended but there was an alternative. We could join an organised cycle tour of the town.. It sounded fun with a visit to the Souk El Had and a ride along the five miles of promenade..We were the last to sign up for the expedition – and Bet was given a small cycle which was a little heavier than the rest. She didn't seem too happy with it but I had no worries. She was a good cyclist and had excellent road sense. Something was wrong. Whenever the group stopped, Bet fell over. She got up each time, seemingly unscathed, and blamed the heaviness of the cycle. I could not understand what was happening. At least five times she crashed to the ground with the cycle on top of her. Apart from a grazed knee she survived intact. At least that is what we thought.

The next year was full of adventure. We moved house; Bet had a garden once more; we flew to Sarawak as guests of my students from way back in 1966 and we planned a holiday in Orkney. All seemed well with our world. Bet, however, was becoming increasingly concerned about her left hand. She was finding it progressively difficult to use her sewing machine, she rarely played the piano now and preparing vegetables seemed to be a growing problem. I noticed that when gardening she would sometimes not be using her left hand. She blamed this onto her falls off the bicycle – which she believed had damaged her left shoulder. By the summer of 2012 her hand was looking visibly misshapen and the fingers were beginning to claw. She went to see her GP and arranged to see a consultant neurologist at Treliske Hospital.

It is clear now, from re reading his letters, that the neurologist was not totally convinced by Bet's insistence that her multiple cycle falls were the cause of her problems, but he arranged an appointment with a hand surgeon with a view to repairing the ulna nerve on her elbow and the median on her wrist. She was offered day surgery on 30th November. I could not understand why she suddenly decided to cancel this. She claimed that her symptoms were improving and that she didn't want to be incapacitated over Christmas. I tried to reason with her. She became anxious and distressed. This was out of character. It was obvious that she was worried at the thought of losing the use of her hand. I knew also that she was worried about her sight. For years she had been fighting herpes in her eye. That had come about just a few days after we were visited by a friend with shingles, and although the medical profession continue to deny any link, Bet felt otherwise. Always into alternative therapies she had taken to herbs and tinctures in order to keep the herpes in a dormant state. She hated taking Acyclovir and blamed that drug on the fact that her memory was sometimes letting her down. Were all these things now combining to Bet's increasing concern and apparent distress?

Early in 2013 she could no longer disguise the fact that her arm and hand were suffering. There was obvious muscle wastage. She accepted that the operation might help and went ahead. She was not happy. Her mind set seemed negative. This was out of character but totally understandable. The surgeon upset her by referring to her 'vintage' years. In the past Bet would have laughed – but now she was bitter and angry. With hindsight I can now see that Bet was losing her ability to smile.

By the end of the year Bet's neurologist had reached a different conclusion. His letter, which Bet would have hidden from me if she could, now gave a clear diagnosis of 'Monomelic amyotrophy' of her left arm. He had explained to her that this was a localised form of motor neurone disease. It can sometimes just stay as a problem for one arm. Sometimes it progresses for a couple of years and then plateaus. It can then remain stable for many years. It is, however, possible for the weakness to advance and to involve other limbs. Bet had not asked me to join her at this consultation and I respected her decision. She did not mention anything that her consultant had discussed with her, merely continuing to blame the surgeon for making her hand worse. A letter from the MND Coordinator followed in the next post. Bet was very troubled. There were tears and anger. There was no way, she claimed, that she could have motor neurone disease. She was in total denial. She had no intention of meeting with the MND Coordinator. I was shocked and baffled. How was I to react? How was I to help? And I knew that Bet had a growing problem with her left leg. She was walking with a definite limp.

I have been through this scenario so many times over the past two years. Why couldn't she talk to me about this? Why did she try to shut me out from her life at this point? What was going on in her mind? How I wish that I could have supported her through what must have been frightening, horrific mental images of a future without hope. Was she protecting me from further trauma? She knew how we had both suffered throughout Becca's fight for survival against all the odds. Was she unable to face the fact that we were about to have to embark on another hopeless journey? Or was it that she was also suffering the early stages of frontotemporal dementia? Denial of any illness is a key symptom of that form of dementia. I will never know – and perhaps it is futile to even try to understand.

Again hindsight enables a degree of possible comprehension. Bet's diaries reveal that before our cruise she was concerned about dizziness and a feeling of vertigo. Could this be a cause of the lack of balance on the bicycle ride? Her diaries disclose anxiety and concern but she never accepts that there could be any link to MND. Her hand and arm problems remained, in her view, a direct result of a cycle that was the wrong size and weight. Her 'clumpy foot', which later weakened her leg, was due to a slip on the roadway. She remained adamant to the end that these problems could be solved by the right chiroprator. She held me responsible for the fact that I never found the right one for her. The one with the magic wand.

"There's too much bloody sugar!"

Friday 25th September 2015 Falmouth
Penmere to Bath Spa

This morning I am catching the 07.53 from Penmere Station. This is the school run. My eleven-year-old grandson Joe may be on the platform – one of those who have elected to travel to Penryn for secondary education as that school has a glowing reputation for 'sport'. I regret the passing of the 'community school' where the comprehensive ideal of 'equal value of each individual' was the guiding philosophy. I made the decision to leave the teaching profession in 1993 when 'league tables' were introduced and the inevitable clamour for so-called 'good' schools was about to distort my beliefs. I had enjoyed thirty years as a teacher – potentially the most rewarding career of all.

I quite expect Joe just to briefly acknowledge me – after all a grandfather can be a bit of an embarrassment. But instead he and his mates come over and chat with a politeness that suggests genuine warmth and affection. My grandchildren have been such a support to me over the past couple of years. I don't suppose Joe will ever forget how 'Bet Bet' – Bet never wanted to be called 'granny' or anything that suggested maturity – had bitten his cheek quite hard when he had closed in to give her a cuddle. She normally dismissed such an action and explained that she had meant it to be a kiss. On this occasion she told him that she had meant to 'cough up phlegm'. In her world where she would openly spit, blow her nose and wipe it on her dress and poke and scratch her vagina whenever she felt the need, this was not an unexpected response. To an eleven-year-old child this was potentially quite disturbing. Both Joe and Katie understood, as far as anyone can, the complexities of the mind. They also knew that Bet could never recover. Joe leaves the train at Penryn station and I am now alone. This morning I feel 'alone'. The train is full and that is why my isolation feels more acute perhaps?

As we approach Truro Station I can see Kenwyn at the top of the hill. The sun is shining. It will be shining into Bet's room and onto the bed which now cradles her poor body. How I wish she was with me now – well and strong again. I reassure myself that Mary will treat her well today when she visits. She will offer her the fruits I have left in the fridge. I then realise that I hadn't mentioned the chocolates in the top drawer. I know how Bet seems to look forward to one of those. How things have changed. My Bet would never have craved sugar as she does now. How would she manage without her chocolate? Today I have left Bet in the care of others and I know that I should not be feeling this guilt.

I am catching the 08.25 from Truro to Paddington and I take a photograph of the train as it approaches the platform. I want to share this journey with Bet. I want to share this more than anything else I have ever wanted to share – a feeling which seems to engulf me. Bet had never been able to visit Joan and Peter in their new home on the Isle of Wight. I am going to see then for the second time and it feels so wrong. Bet and I had always travelled together, sharing the excitement and anticipation of train journeys in particular. There is something very special about train travel. We grew up, of course, in the age of steam where the train was the accepted form of distance travel. As a child I remember journeys in carriages without corridors – and I assume without toilets. How on earth did older people manage with their prostate problems that hadn't yet been diagnosed – it would seem such problems didn't exist in those halcyon days. Perhaps these men didn't travel? I remember trips from Moorthorpe to Sheffield where the railway tracks cut through the steel work yards – with blast furnaces either side. Coming home at night was the nearest one could get to the fires of hell – or so I believed. It was from Moorthorpe that the young teenagers had set forth to work in Skegness and it was by train that Bet had made the daily trip from her farm to share our vague attempt at 'silver service' with the arrogant gangly youth from South Yorkshire who had already stolen her heart. Not that I was to realise this, of course, for a good few years! I had read a travel book about Andorra and I had become fascinated by the prospect of hiking through the Pyrenees. Several of us had vowed to go – but in the end, weeks before I went to college, it was just Bet and I. She shared my love of adventure. This was the start of a journey through life – an odyssey that was to last for over half a century. I remember at about this time, coming across "The Road Not Taken" by Robert Frost. This has remained my favourite poem – almost my inspiration.

Two roads diverged in a yellow wood,
And sorry I could not travel both
And be one traveller, long I stood
And looked down one as far as I could…

Robert Frost

Looking back, our journey to Andorra was quite an achievement – long before Eurostar and Internet booking had even been thought of. We camped and walked, we bathed in cool mountain streams – the same ones maybe that seduced me into smoking "Consulates" those menthol cigarettes that were healthy and 'cleared ones lungs! We both carried a rucksack – and each had a tent. Rucksacks and tents in 1962 were heavy and bulky. It was all so correct in those days. Bet was a friend – and it would have been so wrong of me to assume anything other. As for sleeping together – my mother (and I assume Bet's) had instilled in us the dangers and pitfalls of any suggestion of sexual activity. I think, by that time, I knew the basics of lovemaking – the very basics! It had not been a fast learning experience but I at last knew that I couldn't make a girl pregnant just by holding her hand! Scrambling up the cols of the mountains I did hold Bet's hand. It was confirmation of the fact that she was my best friend. We also did finally and sensibly sleep in the same tent. A cat – or some other wild creature – had found itself trapped in my tent one night and clawed at my face in the pitch black of the mountain valley. Bet moved in to protect me!

It wasn't the only time we had boarded a train as a result of me reading a book. As a teacher one of my favourite books was 'The Boy With a Bronze Axe" by Kathleen Fiddler. How many times I had read out the description of Skara Brae – the Neolithic settlement on the main island of Orkney. How I had hoped to stir in the minds of those eleven and twelve year olds imprisoned before me in the classroom chains, images of wild storms and wind swept foreshores, of beings struggling for survival against a nature which could be violently angry. It wasn't until 2012 that we were to make the journey to the Northern Isles. We used the overnight sleeper up to Paddington – a real touch of romance still. Although now, with my as yet undiscovered prostate problem, I was so glad of the corridor and toilets. Bet, bless her, would always take the top bunk – just to make my nocturnal wanderings just that little bit easier for me. On the east coast line speeding towards Edinburgh we found ourselves sitting opposite a charming lady who lived on Orkney. Bet always felt at ease talking to people – believing that a stranger was just a friend waiting to be discovered. It had led us into some fascinating conversations and some beautiful friendships and surprise, unplanned journeys. Now we had an invitation to coffee on the island and detailed notes scribbled around our OS maps that we had produced from our rucksacks (now a much lighter style – and we were not camping!) Sadly our once speeding train didn't manage the journey without a problem and we arrived in Edinburgh with only a few minutes to catch our connection to Inverness. Oh dear. How one can easily misread! We came to find ourselves heading towards Inverlewe! The guard (or train manager) was helpful and worked out how we could get to Inverness before everything would come to a halt.

Orkney, and in particular Skara Brae and the Ring of Brodgar, did live up to my expectations. Of course the reality is never quite as colourful or as dramatic as the visions created in the technicolour of the mind but I would not allow myself to be disappointed. We hired a car and a cottage at Orphir on the south of the mainland, which overlooked Skapa Flow. We both loved the birds and the unusual wild flowers by the shore line; the Celtic monastery at Birsay only accessible at low tide; the Viking settlements and the related mythology; the dramatic cliffs and boggy terrain of Mull Head – and the wind which permanently seemed to beat against our faces. The landscape could be described, like the architecture, as rather dull and monotonous – and there are few trees and little shelter. I almost lost the car door on many occasions – until I learned to park the Orkney way with the car pointing directly into the wind. The problem then is opening the door to get out of the car. This is, however, a better option – and in the end far cheaper. It is fairly expensive to replace a whole car door and the fine print of the tourists insurance probably doesn't offer too much cover. Driving was, apart from needing to concentrate on wind direction, a pleasure. The roads were good and the traffic very sparse.

I suppose Becca came into our thoughts very often. We knew she would have loved these islands and their remoteness. I always felt guilty, the same guilt as was now amplified by the fact that Bet is no longer by my side as the train crosses the Tamar and I am once again back in England. Bet felt close to Becca wherever we were. She felt her presence, her comfort and often heard her voice. It is only now, with that blessed hindsight, that I wonder whether this was a natural reaction, or whether it was a precursor to Bet's later mental problems – a harbinger of the darkness later to consume us both. We did talk about Becca. It wasn't as though we avoided the tragedy of her death – in fact we had devoted much of our lives now to raising awareness of melanoma. But on Orkney there were special Becca moments' when we both were certain of her presence and her love. We were both transfixed by the peace of Kirkwall Cathedral and its ancient starkness. It had provided protection from whatever the elements could hurl. There, in the solitude and calm, we both felt at peace and this is something I clearly remember sharing. Most of the time though we were two solitary figures out on a bleak landscape – isolated from most of the world. I wish now that I had held Bet's hand more – after all she was still my best friend. It was at these times, when nature seemed at its most feral, that Becca would swirl into our minds. There in the wind and the rain her spirit would be. Orkney was her sort of place and we were there experiencing it partly for her.

At the end of the week we flew up to Shetland. It had seemed a pity to come so far north and not set foot on the most northerly isles. This was to be such a lovely, if fleeting adventure and we vowed to return one day. The fiord-like coast and dramatic landscape captivated us both even though for the two days we toured the main island it was shrouded in mist. We stayed at the Busta Hotel for a couple of nights – and loved the history of the place. Built in 1588 by a Thomas Gifford it claimed its own ghost – a tragic woman searching for her lost son. We wondered how many other poor souls had been lost in the rambling dark corridors as we laughed and giggled our way through the labyrinth of stone – eventually making love when we once again managed to find our room. The wailing of the ancient plumbing set us off again into laughter. We did laugh. We did seem to enjoy life. We had survived the kind of tragedy that often tears couples apart, we had lost a child, and yet, it seemed, we felt strong together.

We used our whole day as the mist cleared to walk across Muckle Roe and appreciated the Hams, the stacks, the red granophyre cliffs and the geos – incredible coastal scenery which brought back distant memories of physical geography lectures at Coventry College of Education where it had seemed I was destined to become a geography teacher. We walked about ten miles and saw no other people. We felt honoured, as we crossed into an isolated bay, to find ourselves sharing the shoreline with a community of seals. They kept a close eye on us but there was no fear. We sat on rocks and they came closer. Apart from the gentle lapping of the water's edge and the sliding of their bodies through the mirror of the sea, all was so quiet. For both of us this would be a serendipitous moment. The walk back was not quite so calming, for, as often happened, I had chosen to leave the trodden path and rely on reading the map. I have led my family to some challenging routes – and this was no exception. We got back to Busta before dark and the search for our bedroom paled the hazards of the intrepid cliffs of Muckle Roe.

The next day we drove down the island as tourists do. We were impressed by the museum in Lerwick; we stopped by the field of Shetland ponies to take photographs; we walked over the isthmus onto St Ninian's Island; we talked for ages with the lovely curator of the Crofter's Museum and finally arrived at Jarlshof – the Viking settlement on the southern point. Here Bet discovered that the custodian had originated in Lincolnshire – not quite a relative but so easily could have been. A night in the rather dour and bleak Sumburgh Hotel and breakfast with the aircrew that would shortly be whisking us over to Edinburgh. Trains are wonderful ways to begin holidays but we always felt, that when such lovely experiences come to a natural end, one should get home as quickly as possible. Pick up the milk and groceries and get the washing machine on, make a pot of tea, sit in one's favourite chair – and begin to reflect! And so we caught a connecting flight to Newquay where our good friends Ann and Kevin were there to collect us.

We had met Ann and Kevin just a few days after we had moved into our flat in Falmouth. From our balcony we had a wonderful view over the river but also an excellent insight into the lives of those who lived in the houses below. We watched Kevin fastidiously completing the final stages of his 'hut'. This was, however, more like an alpine chalet – a beautiful construction. I had watched in admiration as Kevin paid such attention to the finest detail. Here was a craftsman at work. I had envied not only his skill but also the fact that his wife was forever at his side or at the foot of his ladder. I had assumed that she was there to help – although I later came to realise that Ann was there to supervise! I had to pop down and complement him on his work – and our friendship was struck.

Throughout our life in Falmouth, Ann and Kevin have been our closest companions. We have shared much together and enjoyed many 'jollies' as we came to call our walks, drives and train rides into the local area. After our return from the Northern Isles Ann had discovered that the National Trust had a special October Offer of a free pudding with every main lunch course. We were all members and this gave us an excuse for a whole series of 'jollies'. We used the train to Lanhydrock, again to Calstock and a walk to Cothele (where we were quite disappointed to find ourselves charged for the cream which was dolloped on the free pudding). We had to drive to Trerice and Michael's Mount. There the walk over the causeway was worth the effort, for their apple crumble was to be awarded our top marks. It proved great fun and at that point Bet enjoyed the puddings. Sugar was not yet a problem!

We are now approaching Bath Spa Station and I change here for Southampton. Just me. No one else here to help me – or be helped. It seems a long way round but the Internet threw this route out as the cheapest and quickest and I clicked the button and the tickets arrived by the next morning's post. I may not have become a bus conductor but my love of travel still continues. In today's world a young me would be drawn towards a career as a travel agent. After returning from the Northern Isles Bet and I had decided that we ought to explore the Western Isles – after all Benbecula was another island that I had once read about and which had captured my imagination. I now have all the relevant OS maps and have notes about the Mallaig railway and ferries onward to Mull and beyond. I somehow don't think I want to go alone but maybe time will make journeys easier to bear.

Ann has a similar love of timetables and adventure by rail. A year after our excursion to Orkney and Shetland, all four of us this time, were on the night sleeper from Truro to Paddington. The catalyst for this adventure had been Ann's desire to experience the only ferry still in existence where the train actually boarded the boat. We were en route to Sicily. Had we been years younger I could have found myself working alongside Ann in some turmoil of world travel planning, coordinating boats and planes – projecting people to all parts of the globe. The Internet has provided people like us the opportunity to explore the globe. The pegboard timetable still held its fascination! Ann took the lead and did most of the research and booking. I don't find it easy to take a 'back seat' but Ann is quite formidable. Ask Kevin!

I don't have long to wait here in Bath. The Southampton train is a three carriage one – always a disappointment I suppose. I now find Eurostar beginning to feel a wee bit dated. That's how we got to Paris of course and after a picnic lunch in the Jardin des Plantes we crossed back over the Seine and boarded the train onwards to Chur in Switzerland. Bet and I had a rucksack each as usual but Kevin had a suitcase on wheels. I began to sense that Bet was struggling and made envious comments about how we too should have made our lives easier. Early signs that Bet was beginning to struggle physically. There were to be many instances throughout the next two weeks that were out of character. All part of growing older perhaps? That's what happens no doubt. I certainly knew that I was slowing down. It was me who fell as we were walking in the hills around Chur. Bet would seem elated by the fact that she could climb any incline faster than I could and would complain that my breathing had become noisy and laboured. These were early signs of character change that a few months later would strike with such devastation. Never again would I ever experience any form of sympathy or understanding from my once so-loving Bet.

Kevin has a particular penchant for ice cream – one could call him a connoisseur who was now heading for Italy where his wife had planned a route via the most renowned gelateria. I could sense that Bet disapproved in some way. She was far more interested in the culture, I knew she would be happier entranced in the churches – soaking up the history but we had always valued the sheer variety of humanity and enjoyed the fact that we had such an eclectic group of friends. For some unfathomable reason this ice cream trail was beginning to annoy her. I sensed her discomfort, certainly when I too indulged, but was at a loss as how to alleviate her anxiety. Whilst Ann and Kevin relished the local breads and cheeses Bet became fixated on fruit. She carried her plastic bag everywhere – and always a bottle of water and whatever fruit we could pick up in the local shops or markets. By the time we had reached Sicily her contempt for sugar had become obsessional. We stayed in two lovely contrasting 'agroturismo' farmhouses. The first was on the slopes of Etna and the second a few kilometres from Syracuse. Here the Sicilian breakfasts were at their most Sicilian – with sweet biscuits and cake – and not a peach or apple in sight. Bet was at times visibly unhappy. Something was wrong and we couldn't understand why Bet, usually so tolerant and understanding, was getting almost distressed by, and suspicious of food. In the past she had tackled anything and everything with a degree of bravura and enthusiam. The dreaded durian by the roadside in Sarawak just two years previously was just one example of her normal sense of adventure and willingness to discover new tastes.. We had for many years eaten organically whenever we could – for we had discovered how Bet's mum, knocked off her feet by Multiple Sclerosis, had responded so positively when fed with food free from pesticides and other chemicals. We both felt that Con's condition had been activated by aerial crop spraying which had once saturated their farm. Until now though we had accepted the limitations of a chemical free diet and had eaten with a sensible regard for the practicalities of life. It now seemed as though Bet was becoming a slave to her belief and was beginning to condemn me, and our friends, for our love of pistachio ice cream on the slopes of Etna.

This wasn't the only disturbing change that we noticed. We hired a car in Sicily and Kevin and I took turns in driving. On Kevin's day Ann was well prepared with her map and notes. Kevin would be navigated round the tortuous bends and unfathomable mazes of the hillside villages – communities which simply refuse to acknowledge that cars could ever become a necessity in life. Hire cars seem always to be white and I am sure the locals place wagers as to the number of times the same tourist car passes by as they sit in the shade watching their world, bewildered as to why the driver is getting increasingly frustrated by the total lack of any useful signage. On my driving days Bet seemed unable to contribute. Her once impeccable sense of direction no longer existed. She held my notes but her once accurate map reading skills were no longer in evidence. In the past few months I have read her diaries from that time. She was beginning to feel that things were not quite as they had been. She accepts that she is losing some abilities but there is a sense that I am to blame. She observes my lack of patience and my growing annoyance and is unnerved. She begins to doubt our relationship. She is jealous of what she sees as a strong friendship between myself – and Ann in particular. Now in Sicily she would choose to sit in the shade by herself – leaving the three of us cavorting with a beer by the poolside.

I can now begin to trace stages in her growing lack of self-confidence. In 2010 the four of us had become part of the volunteer band who had marched into The Poly offering to help resurrect the floundering Arts Centre. Kevin offered his services as a carpenter, Ann and I agreed to organise the Box Office – and Bet proposed putting her sewing skills into refurbishing all the curtains. We bought a bed sheet from Trago, cut it in half and Bet sewed along the edges. That turned out to be her sole contribution. From that point she would claim that it was more important for her to tend her garden. Meanwhile I threw myself into The Box Office and for the next few years I would spend hours each week – sometimes evening shifts where we were expected to man the front of house until the film had finished. I can now recognise how Bet must have been feeling. It is now obvious that she could no longer use her sewing machine. That skill which had been so much part of our lives was no longer – her left hand was beginning to lose its capacity to hold and manoeuvre. She was now seeing me as uncaring as I spent an increasing amount of time away from home and in the company of others. It looked very much like a catch twenty-two situation as I tried to make sense of what was happening. My frustration, perfectly understandable perhaps, just compounded the insecurities, which were beginning to change Bet's life forever. If I had known, at that point, what was happening – could I have at least alleviated some of the fear and uncertainty that Bet must surely have felt? Before these complex forms of dementia can be diagnosed just what harm are those around their loved ones causing as they laugh, cry and get angered by behaviour they cannot understand or influence?

Ann and Kevin made their return journey by train but Bet and I flew home. We used Ryan Air – my first experience of the cattle truck battle for seating where even those who had paid extra for a particular seat were just flung anywhere in order for the flight to take off on time – and presumably the crew would be paid. Shortly after our jaw-dropping ordeal Ryan Air introduced allocated seats.

On our return from Sicily things did not improve. Bet's obsession with organic food continued to grow. I remember how her illogical insistence on buying organic potatoes had caused us to leave Tesco's empty-handed. She was shouting at me and I couldn't understand why. As I planned my 70th birthday gathering for a weekend in November Bet tried to insist that everyone involved should bring organic food. I had hired a country house and invited twenty guests. Each family was to accept responsibility for one meal and Bet became very angry as I explained that it would be unfair to demand what food should be provided. Part of the fun was to enjoy the surprise and until a few weeks previously Bet would have totally embraced that delight. The gathering noted that all was not well with Bet. She appeared tense and opinionated; she was unable to contribute to the preparation and cooking of our own meal – which happened to be Sunday lunch; and she wasn't smiling any more.

With hindsight I can now remember that Bet sat closely to Ian B after lunch. She was looking at photographs on his computer screen – for Ian had once more accepted the role of our official photographer for this occasion. From that point on Bet was to comment so frequently that almost every view would make a good photograph. She had suddenly assumed the mantle of a photographer's advisor. Ian was to become her fantasy paramour – the gallant hero who would one day rescue her from her world which was rapidly becoming more narrow and threatening. By Christmas his role was confirmed in Bet's mind and I had discovered her making soup as his arrival seemed imminent.

The train is getting close to Southampton. I eat the last remnants of my packed lunch – not that it was ever 'packed' – merely flung into a plastic bag. No sugar though. Not even my favourite Kit Kat! I had avoided sugar. How ironic that I should now be diagnosed as having Type 2 Diabetes.

"Just too much bloody sugar!"

"You're OCD – just like Ian!"

Friday 25th September Bath Central to Southampton

This hasn't been the most exciting journey. There has been no one to talk to and my thoughts have tended to be on a single track. That clickerty-click track which in the past I have found comforting but today it has a dulling monotony. I am travelling alone. Never again will Bet be with me. Not that she is dead. I am not a widower. What an awful word that is. I've never liked 'widow' either. Yet grieving for the loss of a loved one cannot be any worse. I know that. We have lost a daughter and that loss, even though eight years ago, is still as painful as it was at the time. It has changed. One adapts. The mind compensates. And that grief I shared with Bet. I have to cope with this new loss alone. It seems as though I lost Bet two years ago – and yet I have cared for her. I still care for her. How will I feel when she does die? Perhaps she will continue to live in this useless state for months – years perhaps? MND can plateau. The cruel deterioration of the body can slow down. No one can tell me what to expect. What is she like today? What have I done? I have left her in the care of others. I have abandoned her and if I am not careful I know I will be overwhelmed with a futile feeling of guilt. I must focus on my journey. I must, as I have done for many months now, just inhabit the here and now.

The docks signify we are near the sea – although there are non of the dramatic Cornish vistas that will welcome me home. In fact I cannot see any water at all. There are just miles, it seems, of containers stretching for as far as I can see. Our lives are cluttered with so much 'stuff' – things we really do not need. Objects, material things which, at the end of the day, are of no real value. The important things are those who we love – those people who smile at us, who hold our hands and comfort us. And when they have gone what is left?

Thankfully there is Joan – with her huge smile and encompassing arms and I am smiling again and feeling strength from her enveloping hug. Some friends have the ability to lift me from the edge of the void. Joan is one of those saviours. She almost demands that I am buoyant – and yet I know that I can share with her my darkest fears. That strident Glaswegian accent pulls me up – lifts me into a lighter place. Peter arrives – another easy friend with a deep compassion – for he lost his previous partner to cancer and he has real empathy with me. I know I will be safe in their company for the next few days. They will understand if I cry. There will be no embarrassment; no awkward silences. The natural silences will be fine; they will be totally understood and shared. There will be none of the superficial, inane and placatory platitudes that can so often be the well-meaning response of many friends. At times, over this weekend, I know questions will be hard-hitting and emotionally challenging perhaps – but I so prefer that to those situations where friends don't talk about Bet – either for fear of upsetting me or themselves. The interrogation begins immediately as we walk to the car. I know tears are close – but that is understood.

We are driving to Ikea and I recognise that we are now close to Bugle Street. Daughter Sam had been to University in Southampton in 1991. She had studied Archaeology – and as most newly qualified archaeologist do – had started her working life behind a bar. She completed one 'dig' at Buckler's Hard during the summer and then accepted a job at the newly refurbished 'Crown and Sceptre'. This pub was part of the Whitbread chain and the Area Manager, Ian Williams, seemed to pay it particular attention. Most days he would bring in some more bar towels or beer mats and ask for a bacon and egg sandwich. Only when Sam declared that she couldn't cope with any more Whitbread paraphernalia and bar towels were piled as high as the bar itself did she discover Ian's motives. He was trying to pluck up the courage to ask her out! Ian had a house in Bugle Street, right beside the city walls, and it wasn't long before Sam moved in there.

Bet and I visited several times – eaves dropping in on a world which seemed to consist of 'Stella Parties' and midnight runs, naked along the city walls. High ranking medical consultants and police officers they now might be – but they once looked pretty silly! We enjoyed their company as a carefree life beckoned them.

Into Ikea we go. I'm not sure whether I have been into this one. They are all the same aren't they? I certainly remember the one in Bristol where Ian and Sam, having long moved from Southampton, had chosen their new kitchen. We had to return several times, as Sam needed to change various specifications. She has never been one for quick decisions and this was no exception. Thankfully we realised that by entering the second wardrobe on the right on the first long aisle we could save a good six hundred yards. The Narnia moment took us directly into a magic world of dishwashers and waste disposal units.

Bet and I had never owned a dishwasher until very recently. Only last year when I had rented a level ground floor flat for a few months had we had the use of one. By that time of course I was totally responsible for 'washing up' although Bet would make me feel guilty if I ever used it. Before that we had always shared the task. I say always, but there were many years when it would have been shared only at weekends. As I reflect back over our lives together I realise how much time Bet must have spent on feeding the children, on cleaning our homes and on surrounding us with care and love. Little wonder that now she would be resentful of the fact that those loving, all encompassing labours, were no longer within her capability. For the past two years all those tasks in which she had taken such pride had grown beyond her and she now watched on as I took them over. She was initially critical of everything I cooked. There was not enough taste; the gravy was too thin; the vegetables were undercooked or overcooked; and my failures were readily broadcast to anyone who came to visit. My meals were always ravenously devoured however – and in the early stages of Bet's illness food would be shovelled. Table manners seemed irrelevant. Entertaining friends to supper could have been an embarrassment had I not had such challenging situations as a young boy. Later I would need to feed her and swallowing difficulties would mean a change to her diet – but for 2014 it was a question of maintaining a varied intake of good nutritious food and for washing up without daring to use the dishwasher. There always seemed to be the almost logical inference that Bet had cooked for the forty-six industrious years of our marriage – and now it was my turn.

Perhaps the same feelings were dictating how she reacted to washing – although here there were puzzling and totally illogical aspects. Bet had always set high personal standards of cleanliness – and although she continued to want a daily shower and hair wash – she no longer saw the need to wash clothes. Her new method of eating meant dribbles and splashes would cover her top and skirt – but she would never accept that this was a problem. She was in denial again and unable to accept that she had now become a 'messy pup'! It must have been unbearably hard to accept that she could no longer achieve even the simplest of tasks? Little wonder the brain refuses to acknowledge such changes. The new reality is that one's clothes are fine and that the food splatterings are inconsequential. For weeks it became a battle as I would argue a case for a change of clothes. Bet became attached (almost literally) to a favourite purple top and a multi-striped skirt which she had bought a year previously from Sea Salt. The skirt became a particularly irritating problem for me. After a month of arguments and frustrations as the said garments were washed, dried and back on between nightfall and sunrise I had a 'eureka' moment. I helped Bet into the car and on our daily sojourn around the villages and back along the scenic drive to Pendennis Point we stopped outside Sea Salt's Factory shop. I asked the sales girl just to pop outside and meet my wife – and in particular to note her skirt. Bet must have been very puzzled by my behaviour but it did mean that I could buy another two identical skirts and that particular problem was solved.

It was when the ironing board came out that Bet really appeared rattled.

"You're just like Ian!" she would sarcastically sneer at me from her chair.

Ian routinely irons his work shirts on a Sunday evening. He has a shirt for every day and these are usually good quality cotton – far more expensive than the non-iron variety Bet had washed for me over my working years. So why had I started to iron at this stage of our lives? There was a touch of pride I suppose. If I was now responsible for Bet's appearance then I wanted her to be as clean and tidy as I could present her. I had also inherited a few of Ian's old shirts – rescued from plastic bags en route to charity shops. I'm not proud!

I had the same response whenever I cleaned down

the kitchen work surfaces. Ian does this, again as a matter of compulsive routine after the family evening meal. Now he owns 'The Cavendish Coffee House' in town he sets the highest standards in table cleanliness. His 'five star' hygiene record is well deserved.

"He's over the top!" Bet would frequently observe. "And now you are just like him!"

Whenever the vacuum cleaner came out I would suffer further verbal abuse.

"Why are you cleaning again? It doesn't need cleaning! You are worse than Ian!"

Several times over the past two years I have tried to bring in help with domestic tasks – an excuse for a few hours of 'freedom'. I shiver now as I think back to the problems my creative and devious plans have caused. Mary, a lovely young friend of Sam's was the most successful of my band of potential helpers. Most got very abusive reactions and eventually we decided mutually to terminate our brief experiments. Mary, however, was accepted by Bet and came to help 'clean' for a few hours each week. Mary is visiting Bet now and I wonder if she has discovered the chocolate in the top drawer. I give myself a shake. This is my free time now and I must value it. It is what I have craved for the past two years. There should be no feeling of guilt.

I am walking behind Joan and Peter. They are heading for the picture frames. Peter paints – some lovely work – and Joan manoeuvres him gradually towards her view of a more commercial style. She is now obviously going to make final decisions as to how his work should be framed. Even eves dropping on this scene I am saddened. I am no longer part of a pair. Well I am – but my partner must inevitably leave everything to me. I feel so alone again. I look at the display of mirrors and wander off through piles of cushions stacked high. Back to the useless clutter of our lives. The containers in the docks; the litter of western society's so-called needs; the brash greed of a city. Bet yearned to live again in the depths of the countryside. She would not be happy here.

Bet was born on August 19th 1944 – and christened simply Betty Dowse. Her dad was Walter Henry and her mum Constance Iris. They rented Gorse Farm at Fulletby on the edge of the Lincolnshire Wolds. Two years ago Bet had become quite obsessional about collating her childhood memories and she had asked me to type them out for her. I made a booklet and added photographs. I am so glad that I did this – for it has proved invaluable for medical staff and carers in the past few months. It saddens me that not one of our support team knows my Bet. A glance at her "Childhood Memories" at least gives a brief insight into a life once full of laughter and joy.

By the time I met Bet in Skegness her mum and dad now owned their own small eight acre farm "The Poplars" at Monksthorpe near Spilsby. I clearly remember my first visit. Walter, a lovely gentle gentleman, picked me up in his Austin pickup which seemed to be held together with farm twine. Con was there in the lovely warm kitchen. There was a tangible happiness and I felt immediately relaxed, welcome and 'at home'. I remember that the farm house was furnished with a hotch potch of basic items which Con had collected at local sales. There was little that seemed new – although everything seemed to be valued and functional. This family was poor in material terms – yet so rich in self-sufficiency and self-confidence. They were totally happy with their lot. There was never any suggestion that others had anything remotely worthy of envy. When 'Swannee' the Postman called a plate of fried bacon and egg would be placed before him – even though he may have had nothing to deliver. I visited the farm whenever I could. They had my wellies by the door and I joined in the farm activities wherever I could. I like to think that I became just a part of the family. Bet wasn't my girl friend – she was my friend. I don't think she saw it that way and would later claim that she played a waiting game and eventually I fell into the trap!

I remember that fall! My Mum and Dad were taking me to Heathrow where I was to fly – in a BOAC Comet no less – to Singapore and then on to Sarawak. We spent a night at Bet's farm and my parents met Walter and Con. It was warm and comforting as usual; a natural ease. We set off early the next morning for London. I remember how desolate I felt as we drove away from the farm. As I waved to Bet as she disappeared into the distance I felt grief I suppose – a strange feeling that it would be at least a year before I would see her again. We had lunch in Harrow with my girl friend at that time. She was a lovely girl and didn't deserve how cruelly I was to treat her. On the plane I found myself in an emotional turmoil. It wasn't just about the fact that I was embarking on the adventure of my life time but it was about leaving behind Bet, the farm and her mum and dad. In a strange way it seemed more of a loss to be leaving Bet than to be leaving my own family. Bet was my closest friend. I think, by the time I had reached Singapore, via Cairo and Karachi, it had dawned on me that I could marry my best friend. Then I worried that I might be too late. Bet had other boy friends. There was no quick way – but as soon as I could I wrote to her asking if she would marry me! My darling wrote back immediately. I had fallen!

Initially I suspect that my mother may have been a little disappointed with my decision – after all a girl friend in Harrow who had her own car indeed – would in my mother's eyes have been quite a catch. I did behave so badly towards my lovely London girl – and I hope, eventually, that she was able to forgive me.

I came home and Bet was waiting for me. I had brought back a simple silver ring made from an Indian rupee by a roadside crafter in Chiang Mai, Northern Thailand. We were 'engaged' and despite the fact we were living through the 'Swinging Sixties' we behaved fairly properly. I know Bet and I lost our virginity on a beautiful red rug at The Speech House in the Forest of Dean. We returned many years later but couldn't trace the rug! The physical side of our love was always an integral part of our relationship – and indeed continued until the last couple of years. Over

Christmas of 2013 Bet's desire to make 'liebe' (as she would always write in her diary) became insatiable. I would be hurled onto the bed and contortions demanded. This was the stuff of dreams – except for the fact that I was suffering from a fairly advanced form of prostate cancer, not that I knew that at the time. A few months later of course, I was chemically castrated – injected as the first part of my treatment. That coincided with Bet's paranoid feelings that I was about to kill her – and our 'liebe' came to an end. Lovely memories remain – making love under the stars on many occasions – and one very impromptu session in the forest above Cloughton. Only afterwards did we read the signs warning us of the increasing adder population. Not to worry. I know from my jungle treks that snakes avoid vibrations.

We were so thrilled by our first home together. It was a brand new three bed roomed detached house in Thorpe Audlin. It cost us £2700 and we arranged a mortgage which was based on two and a half times our joint salaries. Those were the rules at that time and one can argue that those rules should have stayed. Bet had a teaching post at Upton First School (The pioneering West Riding had newly reorganised into a three tier – First, Middle and Upper School system) where she taught in the reception class. It was a challenging role for at five years old many children came with very limited language skills' "'Ere's a tanner! Get thee sen some chips" was often the limit of parental involvement. Within the year Bet had earned promotion and she became Head of the first two years leading a team of five or six teachers most of whom had been teaching far longer. As far as we know they were happy to have Bet's guidance – and she tackled the job with a quiet confidence that became her hallmark.

I, on the other hand, blundered my way into Cudworth (Cud'erth) Secondary Modern School which seemed to have been left isolated by the West Riding's ground-breaking reorganisation. I remember clearly my telephone conversation with the local education office. I had just returned from Sarawak a day before Christmas 1966 and I needed a job – just for a few months until I could sort myself out. I had no intention of staying in South Yorkshire for I was now a fully-fledged 'adventurer'! When asked what subject I taught I said it was 'English'. That was true of course for I had been the only English person in Chung Hua in Sarawak and much of my work had been with a delightful Transition Class where 11, 12 and 13 year olds came in from the Ulu (jungle) primary schools with only a very limited smattering of English. In one year the aim was to raise the standard of English to the point where all teaching could be carried out in that language. I know the main subject in my three year teacher training course had been 'Geography' – but I avoided any mention of that as I talked with the Education Officer. And so I went into Cudworth to work for Mary Oxley. Mrs Oxley was the first woman head to work in a mixed secondary school and she ruled accordingly and in keeping with the times. I remember Mary's favourite story :

When I came into this school I knew I had to make my mark. I went into the corridor and there were two boys walking down the corridor. I marched them into my office. I think they were trying to tell me that they were on an errand – but I made it clear that I didn't want anyone to be out of the class. I caned them both and asked them to wait outside. I listened behind my door.

One said to the other, "Eh up! She hurts like a fella!"
I knew from that moment that I would be fine!

Mary Oxley c 1965

Somehow, despite all my reservations, and the total shock of finding that teachers in England didn't have the god-like status of those in the Chinese system, I was to stay there four years. Thankfully, by the end of that time, corporal punishment had been banned from schools. By that time also, Bet was being advised to apply for Primary Headships and I was searching for a Head of English (!) post. (I must add that I was also just about to complete an OU degree in English Literature and Education – for I had now decided that was where my heart lay) Which of us was successful first was to determine our next home.

I became Head of English at Foulstone High in Darfield – a newly created comprehensive school and, although Mary Oxley seemed genuinely upset by the fact that I was leaving her school, she introduced us to a friend who had just built some lovely bungalows at Hemingfield. The view was quite awesome – over a valley to the newly landscaped slag heaps. Alpine almost – certainly as the trees began to grow. It was here that our lovely girls were born – Rebecca on March 24th 1972 and Samantha on 17th July 1973. We worked so hard on our garden transforming a steep slope of builder's rubble into a work of art – tiered, landscaped, structured and full of colour. It was an adventure playground for the two toddlers as they negotiated the steps and pathways in order to reach the sand pit in the bottom corner or stroke the horses over the fence in the field below. Bet had now become a full time mum and was a natural. She was so calm about everything and always so patient. She was forever industrious – searching out ways to make our home more comfortable. There was the Buckflex Factory (a kind of synthetic leather) a mile away and Bet soon discovered that she could pick up off cuts very cheaply. Off she would go with her two chicks heaped onto our second-hand push chair, up the hill to the factory, returning with layers of brightly coloured material. Soon our children were dressed in Buckflex coats and pinafore dresses and Bet was making Buckflex toys for family and friends. We must have bought some clothes for our children. Bet surely didn't make everything?

A few years later and we moved to Scarborough where I became Head of Arts Faculty at The Graham School – the one with Hilda Briggs in charge and the massive peg board timetable. Another brand new house in Burniston. We were so pleased to be by the sea and this was such a good place to bring up our young daughters. It was here that Bet found herself in charge of EFL (English as a Foreign Language) in Scarborough's schools and colleges. Initially she would take two Chinese girls, newly arrived from Hong Kong and with very little English, on shopping trips round the local market. They responded well to her calm and caring approach and Bet's ability was soon recognised and she was appointed to the Education Team. It was in Scarborough that I was to begin writing musicals; that Becca was to learn to play the clarinet; that Sam was to struggle in her sister's shadow and that Bet's creative ideas began to take on a more commercial facet and her spiders were to become the talk of the town.

Another move to Filey Road. This was to give us a sea view but, more importantly, provide us with a fourth bedroom so that we could look after my grandmother – now almost blind – and living in a caravan over in Lancashire. She wasn't our first house guest. Back in Hemingfield we had looked after Yong from Sibu. The little boy who had helped me so much over in Sarawak came to stay with us to study A levels. In Scarborough Bet had brought home one of her Chinese students. Jackie Tam was to live with us for a year whist her family could find roots in England. Guests were always welcome and Bet's generosity knew no bounds. Just as her mum had placed a breakfast in front of her vistors, Bet did the same without question.

It was with our move in 1984 to Cornwall that we really became an extended family. We found 'Rylands' at Altarnun, on the edge of Bodmin Moor and that became our home for the next twenty years. Bet's mum and dad, my mum and Pauline, and the four of us were now living in the collection of converted barns in an acre of garden. Bet was truly happy here. I think everyone was. Becca continued to develop her music; Sam rode out of her sister's shadow on the backs of a motley collection of Mandy's horses; Walter discovered bowls and Bet created 'Bits o'Fluff". Sadly after twenty years we needed to move on again. The elders had passed on, the children had fled the nest, and we could no longer afford to maintain the chocolate box dream.

We moved to Bodmin. My mum, the only other person for whom we felt responsible, now needed more care and that's what we willingly wanted to provide. Our house in Bodmin was modern, individually designed and very close to ASDA – the 24 hour super store. We felt we had come the full circle. When we were first married we were possibly two of ASDA's first customers – their very first 'super market' was at South Elmsall – just a few hundred square feet with minimal shelving and stacked boxes. Associated Dairies also opened their first petrol station in Cudworth – just round the corner from the school. It was there, every Friday evening, that I would fill up the A35 for £1.00. And IKEA hadn't yet hit our shores.

On our move to Bodmin we bought new furniture. A local 'fine quality' store was closing its Bodmin branch and we went in and bought virtually all of their window display. Never before had we done such a thing. Never before had we had the spare cash to fund such extravagance. Rylands had created a new wealth and for a brief period in our lives we explored the sensations of buying. Such happiness is a thin veneer of course – and within months I had lost my Mum and we then had to watch on as Becca was to die. Cruel reminders of the real values of life.

Since then we have lost heart in terms of property. A home has become the place where we put down our bags. We have become experts in the art of down-sizing. Our move to the flat was marred by our unhappiness there. Then we 'escaped' to Arwenack Avenue, where after a brief period of once again creating a garden, Bet was to suffer the onset of her problems. We moved to a ground floor flat where steps could no longer hinder Bet's deteriorating ability to walk and then finally onto our present bungalow in Roscarrack Gardens – purpose built for wheel chair access. Even now I am contemplating moving – back into town where I would no longer need a car and where I could walk to the beaches, to M&S and to the cinema. Bet missed the ease of the town so much – but then Falmouth is not really like a town. Down every 'ope' one can see the sea; from every hill one can view the surrounding comfort of productive fields and beautiful coastline; and a fresh wind makes one feel alive. Bet, my country girl, was happy here – or so I thought.

I look back now over the years. Although we have always had functional homes they have always been comfortable and welcoming. The warmth of Bet's childhood stayed with her and the capacity to create loving surrounds without the need for much money.

I like to think that we passed that competence down to our children. I remember how annoyed Sam had been with me one day when I was critical of the house where a friend lived. There were panes of glass missing from the window and sheep by the fire – but to Sam this was a friend's home and that family existed on little money. I was wrong to be casting judgement and she reminded me of that! It was Sam who had asked if I could drop her well-before the school gates when I had a new car. It was embarrassing for her to be seen as affluent in any way – and it was only a Ford Sierra! How difficult she must find her life now – when Ian, impulse buyer that he can sometimes be, orders a 50" TV set and drives a BMW.

In that respect at least, I am not at all like Ian!

"Not the Daily Mail! Please not the Daily Mail!"

Saturday 26th September 2015
Bembridge Isle of Wight

What a glorious day. Not a cloud in the sky and I am sitting on a sun-lounger in Joan and Peter's garden. Through half-closed eyes I sense that Joan is pouring me a glass of wine. It is far too early but I already feel transported, swaddled in a comfort cocoon and away from reality. This place is warm – and the sun, today, is a friend. Oh that it had always been so. Melanoma echoes. For so many years now it has cut deep into my being. Melanoma killed Becca. Not even the glass of wine is going to take away the pain is it? And just to compound my growing fears that my mind will now be flooded with unbearable memories, Joan is reading her copy of the 'Daily Mail'.

After Becca's death on 29th May 2007 Judy Lacy, an old friend of Bet's from school days and now a free-lance medical journalist, wrote a beautifully balanced article on Becca's illness and on her fight for survival. She hoped that it would be snapped up by The Guardian but instead the rights were bought by the 'Daily Mail'. My heart sank. My mother had always read that paper and every day for many years Bet and I had begrudgingly collected it from the village newsagent and lamented on the headlines as

80

we walked back to Rylands along the Cornish lanes. There began a predictable dialogue with the editorial team. The balance, as far as they were concerned, had to be slewed. In some way a dramatic headline had to be created. Either we were expected to condemn the NHS team who had initially left Becca without hope and then clobbered her with bouts of stereo tactic radiation which blasted her brain tumours into painful and potentially lethal haemorrhages – or we should pour scorn onto Dr C whose naturopathic and holistic treatments had given hope but had cost a considerable amount of money. Bet and I could not allow either bias. Bet, particularly, always held a respectful disregard for sections of the medical profession – feeling that medical science was in danger of missing the fact that diet was crucial. The alternative pathway was, in her eyes, the only way Becca could be saved. The Mail arranged a photographer but even he had been given a firm agenda. Bet and I wanted to stress our positive way forward and the fact that we were now campaigning to raise awareness of the dangers of sun burn but the 'Daily Mail' had other ideas and wanted us close to tears. The negotiations went backwards and forwards for several weeks, the summer began to fade, and eventually the paper did not print. I suspect there are many families who have their heart break extended by a press that demands sensationalism.

The red wine is pleasant. The sun is warm on my skin. I was forty years old when a friend, Herbie, raised his eyebrows at a mole on my arm which was becoming darker, larger and blotchier. Now so obviously a danger sign but thirty years ago nothing of great concern – but, nevertheless, I did get myself referred to a specialist in dermatology. It was all very swift – for Cornwall County Council had a very reasonable private health package for employees. Within days the mole had been taken away and the biopsy revealed a malignant melanoma. That was the bad news. The good news was that they were sure that they had removed sufficient tissue and we had caught the demon in time. They were equally sure that it was directly related to a bad sunburn on that arm almost twenty years previously and I remember the occasion so vividly. Sitting on the prow of a Chinese launch, slowly chugging through the Kut canal between the Rejang River and the South China Sea, I had been fascinated by the probiscus monkeys gazing down on this chattering collection of eager Chinese students and their white teacher. The tropical sun made its mark – a very red and painful one. That was the cause, my dermatologist firmly believed, of my now potentially lethal skin cancer. If only the medical team who dealt with me had been equally sure that there was a very high risk that genetic factors were at play – especially as my mother had auburn hair and plenty of freckles! I might have begged my children to take more care. Oh how I wish that I had!

"Just look at this!" Joan waves the Daily Mail. " You can tell whether your partner is faithful or not by the look in their eyes!"

That's all I need. A reminder that Bet has lost all

faith in me and for the past year has accused me of having affairs with everyone we know. I play Joan's game and get a very low score. Am I taking this seriously? Not really! The wine still tastes good. The sun is bright. It glistens sharply. I know my eyes are watering.

I remember so clearly when Becca asked my opinion about the mole on her thigh. Such moments seem engraved for all time. Out of all the millions of images recorded on my brain I will never forget this one. I knew. I saw then her death. It would be years down the line of her life – but it was inevitable. That I knew as soon as my eyes recorded the distorted, multi coloured, murderous mole. I remember how I clutched at straws.

"You have never been badly burned there?" I professed with a vain hope.

" I have dad. When I went wind surfing in Brittany. On the school exchange."

That was over ten years previously. Since then Becca had studied Performance Arts at Middlesex, had set up her theatre company 'Small Scale' with her best mate Donna, and had a partner Steve and an ever-growing collection of musical instruments with which she created fun and fantasy. Becca and Donna had returned with their BAPA degrees and initially created a comedy act 'Washerwomen in Wet Suits' which would tour the pub circuit. Bet and I witnessed their premier in the Stable Bar at The White Horse Inn in Launceston. The venue was crowded and the reaction was wild. The pair certainly had something very special. They were funny – hilariously funny – but they could also sing and play music. I thought that they could 'go far'! I'm not sure which of the duo felt unsure about the comedy circuit but there was a change of direction. They decided that they would set up a community theatre in North Cornwall and eventually Small Scale forged heart warming links with youth groups, old people's homes, schools and hospitals until eventually they seemed to become an integral part of this rural life. They created their own shows – delightful yet perceptive stories full of music, comedy and pathos. And then there was 'Equal Riots"! That was something very special. They worked with those who had learning difficulties and created performances which they took out 'on tour'. Wheel chairs (and their occupants) came into chorus line on cue; physical signs of cerebral palsy subsided when the microphone was held; delightful characters with Downs Syndrome claimed stardom in the spotlight; audiences wiped away tears of laughter and admiration and in the midst was Becca with beaming smile and an accordion – or a clarinet – or the keyboard – or something else that made music such fun. How could someone with such vitality and joy for living be struck down with melanoma? Life just isn't fair sometimes. Shit! That's an understatement!

I wish I could report that Becca's mole had been removed with the same speed and competency that mine had been. Sadly I no longer was teaching and the County had long since given up with the perk of private health care. I did offer to pay for Becca's treatment privately and how I now wish that I had done so. Becca insisted that all would be well and that her GP would deal with it quickly. A week later I was to question why no referral had been received. Becca returned to her GP to discover that the doctor had 'forgotten' to send in the relevant information. I wish that was the only error in the system but a more alarming delay was to follow.

Two weeks later and Becca had her mole removed in Tavistock Hospital and a follow-up appointment made for the following week. The hospital rang a few days later to cancel this appointment and to re book it for the following week. This seemed a strange decision but for a few days I thought positively. Surely if the mole had been malignant and its roots deep, then the appointment would never have been postponed? How wrong I was! And how cruel and thoughtless had the administration been! When Becca eventually did see her surgeon he was very angry with her. He accused her of missing her appointment. The mole was malignant and its roots were deep – far deeper than the incision made a fortnight previously. More flesh had to be gouged out of her leg. The result was a mess and nerves badly damaged beyond repair but hopefully her life would be saved. I still doubted. Somehow I knew that melanoma would take away this happy, loving and creative joy.

The standard test for the spread of melanoma is a six-monthly watch on lymph glands – and Becca's lymph glands never did show any signs of swelling. For the next five years I am sure the medics were thinking that they had successfully gained another tick in the box of cancer survival. Donna left 'Small Scale' to have her children and Becca continued alone for a year before stunning Bet and myself by telling us she was going to become a primary teacher. We were obviously pleased. This would mean a 'proper profession' and a 'salary'! We had watched Becca and Donna struggle for years with little financial reward. My mother too was thrilled! Becca would now be following the family tradition. She worked furiously hard for her year at Marjon's in Plymouth; she was appointed to teach Years One and Two at nearby Lewannick Primary School and all seemed good. But suddenly her partner Steve couldn't handle the stress (or whatever) and left. Becca was so distraught and seemed not to be able to understand. I can still hear her cries through the walls of the flat which Becca and Steve shared next to us in the labrynth of cottage that was 'Rylands'. I hear them whenever I now cry. Whenever I scream aloud for Bet (and Becca) to come back to me.

Becca turned to a close friend, Kev, to try to piece together what had gone wrong. He was truly a very loving companion and she found such comfort as their relationship grew. He gave her the strength to begin teaching and supported her; they made music together and slowly they both realised that something very special was growing from a warm secure mutual respect. Bet and I bought a house for Becca in Launceston. We had sold Rylands and for the only time in our lives we had cash to spare. The idea had been to invest in Becca's house and she could repay us over our life time. This would be a boost to our pensions. That was the theory! Kev was in the final years of a Fine Art Degree at Exeter University and they began to plan a future together where drama, music and art could inspire and motivate others. There was fun and vision. They would become a pair. Their relationship seemed to be taking them to a place beyond the stars. They seemed supremely happy. And Becca had a salary!

Just a few days after my mum had died, and Bet and I had been able to spend time together again, we were invited by Becca and Kev for a meal on the Saturday evening. We decided that we would go over to Exeter in the afternoon to see Kev's final exhibition. His degree was now completed, and not only had he now been awarded his well-deserved B.A., but he had also been selected to receive the prize for landscape painting. We were proud. He is a lovely lad and he was making our daughter so very happy. Vast black and white abstract canvases left a lasting impression – sadly they have become part of a nightmare collage where our laughter was to turn to tears. My mobile rang. And it was Kev's voice. He seemed distressed but with that kind of voice which is trying to reassure the listener that all is well. There was a problem. Becca has just collapsed and the ambulance men were with her. I could hear their voices asking her if she could hear them – that familiar routine! He was sorry! Supper would have to wait. He would phone us from the hospital.

How helpless I felt! My daughter was in trouble and I was unable to hold her and protect her. I didn't know then that I would have to come to terms with my foreboding fear so many times over the next two years. And again, now. Bet lies in her nursing home bed. What the hell am I doing with a glass of wine and a smile on my face hundreds of miles away!

Bet and I drove home almost silently that early summer evening. The landscapes from the A30 can be stunningly beautiful. Dartmoor, enchantingly haunting from a distance but darker and more chilling as one by-passes Okehampton; the tree-topped hill that means there is just a few minutes of driving to cross the Tamar into Kernow and climb towards Launceston with its silhouetted castle and mystical sky line; and a few miles further that wide panoramic collage of ever changing field patterns which seem to stretch forever to Brown Willy, Rough Tor and far beyond and finally Bodmin Moor itself. I shiver at the best of times as I cross this bleak reminder that nature is still in command – but on this night I must have felt totally empty – completely drained of any feelings.

The phone call came. This was the first of so many over the following two years where I dreaded picking up the receiver. Kev has a calm reassuring voice – a quality that I was to appreciate so much as, nail by cruel nail, Becca's fate was to be sealed. She was comfortable and there had been no further seizures. The initial diagnosis seemed to be that she was showing signs of epilepsy but now she was to rest. Kev was to stay there with her and there was no need for us to make the journey down to Plymouth. Over the next two years the pair were to work so hard to protect Bet and myself from as much heart-break as they could.

In hospital Becca had asked one doctor if her seizure could be related to melanoma but he dismissed this as highly unlikely. A brain scan had been reserved for Monday morning but yet again unthinking bureaucracy was to cause inexcusable delays. Becca was offered the option of going home on Sunday morning. She jumped at the opportunity of course – and in so doing she sacrificed her chance of the brain scan. She was now on a waiting list and the suggested waiting time was two months. I remember how furious I was but how I could not allow my anxiety to show. It was better, perhaps, that both Becca and her mum felt reassured by the lack of concern being shown. She still had headaches, very severe headaches, and was told not to return to teaching until it was clear that the 'epilepsy' was under control. I know I didn't share my anxiety with Bet. I never disclosed my feelings that melanoma would take Becca away from us. I would like to think that Bet and I shared our anxieties and grief – but with hindsight I don't think we did. When, eventually a brain scan revealed two brain tumours, one operable and one not, we probably dealt with the next two years in very different ways. When Becca's skilful brain surgeon had spent six hours removing the largest tumour he had to break the news to her and Kev that it was metastatic melanoma, that there was no cure, and that she had two months to live.

How difficult was that next phone call to make? Becca broke the news to us herself. She tried not to cry – but I knew tears were streaming down her face. We were armed. Bet had always followed 'alternative forms' of medicine and through 'Cancer Active' (a charity which I would recommend) we had read about Dr C based in Harley Street – a conventional doctor who had become a naturopath and had gained a good reputation for successfully tackling 'untreatable cancers'. I wasn't convinced but Bet was. This would give Becca hope. The NHS had left her with nothing! Becca and Kev went up to London and, with a terrific thunderstorm echoing around them, met Dr C and came away with the hope they had yearned for. There were some good phone calls! Not all news was bad!

I dealt with my fears by throwing myself fully into sourcing and funding Becca's new programme of diet and healthy lifestyle. I made phone calls to Europe and America. Supplements came from all over the world. I made complex timetables of pills, potions and herbal drinks – and Kev made sure that Becca's regime was followed with precision. His brief spell in the army had stood him in good stead. Her diet was organic and demanding but the pair of them faced the routine with enthusiasm and hope. Whilst I protected myself hiding with the computer, telephone and printer, Bet had less to shelter behind. Looking back I now realise that she must have been far more exposed to Becca's actual reality. She had no shield, no defence. Only the firm belief that Becca's treatment would save her life.

Mr P says her tumour is aggressive and she may only have a short time to live ... Kev was just staring into space. I don't know how they'll cope. We've rung Dr C's clinic but we can't talk to anyone until tomorrow morning. Pete thinks Becca may do nothing – but that would be unthinkable. You have to fight. Dr C sounds unconventional. That will suit Becca. It is so hard to talk to anyone. We just burst into tears. I just don't know what to do. It's just so intolerable. We'll have to do sudukos all night – we just can't cry.
Betty Kaye 22nd August 2005

We did become 'suduko' addicts – and Bet continued to beaver away at her family history research. I hadn't realised, until I read Bet's diaries quite recently, that my doubts were visible to her. But then, we knew each other so well. Or did we?

I really feel isolated sometimes. Pete is so strange. I suppose I'm just not that interesting really except in bed. It's not really that bad – but sometimes I can't take it.
Betty Kaye 9th September 2005

Mr P rang Becca again this morning and suggested that she went back on the steroids but she doesn't want to. I don't really know what to do. I'm a bit redundant in the scheme of things .. so I am writing this diary ...
Betty Kaye 20th October 2005

There was concern here about our relationship. Bet obviously feels that I had grown distant. Was this a recent doubt – or had Bet felt inadequate for sometime? Ten years on and she tells me every day that I don't really love her. There are dormant seeds perhaps lying beneath the surface and now, when 'dementia' peels back the veneer of social propriety, the truth comes out? Or was this a natural reaction to the stress we were both feeling? And so Bet continued to write everyday – and the harrowing detail is there on every page.

> *Becca rang in a terrible state. Dreadful headaches again. The blind spot is still there. her gums are terribly sore, her mouth full of ulcers. She is considering going back on the steroids again. She is starting all the new stuff tomorrow. They are all working it all out. What a lot there is. I tried to do some distant healing and rang Frances for some prayers…*
> *Betty Kaye 22nd October 2005*

Bet maintained faith in her crystals and in the mind's power to heal. In the early stages she worked with Becca on visualisation techniques. Bet never discussed these with me in any detail but I knew that the pair of them would share their images.

> *Had an awful night but visited the black monkey again … I chopped off his head .. not in a frenzy but in a cold-blooded manner with intent.*
> *Betty Kaye 5th August 2005*

Sam, Ian and little Joe joined us all for Christmas. We followed Becca's diet of course so it was 'different'

– colourful roasted organic vegetables smothered in herbs. The presents too had taken an interesting direction – with an enema kit, some very alternative CD's and an extremely large steamer. And on into 2006…

Bet's diaries continue to detail how Becca was feeling every day. Every headache, stomach pain, every swelling and skin blotch, every sickness and fear, every hope and every prayer. The journey was unbearably difficult for us both to observe. I still focused on my 'purpose'. I continued to email, telephone and write. We established an on-line blog – www.beccabob. blogspot.co.uk and all Becca's friends kept in touch. Many of them would ask how best to help and so, half way through 2006 I set up "Becca's Angels" – a fund which would help us to meet the cost of Becca's treatment. I used "Angels" in the theatrical sense – financial backers who would keep 'the show on the road'. The response was beyond all our hopes. Within days £20,000 had been deposited into the 'Angel' account – and this was to double by the end of the year.

I cannot revisit this period of my life. It is too painful. It was unbearable at the time – and now it is impossible. For Bet too of course :

I am so scared for her. Is the treatment on her feet any use? Am I causing this filthy cancer to spread? She is so pale and full of pain. I just want to hold her and take it all away and I can't. For heaven's sake! I am her mother and I should be able to do it! I have prayed

to everyone I can think of and nobody has heard. Kev has tried so hard and it's gone nowhere. She has suffered for almost two years – such awful suffering. It is such an obscene thing – malignant melanoma ....
Bet Kaye 7th April 2007

And from the blog :

To all Becca's Angels 30th May 2007
We are sorry to report that Becca finally gave up her fight against melanoma. She died yesterday evening at home – with Kev and ourselves by her side.

Of course no one wanted this to happen. There is no romantic glow to any of this story. However, two years ago when Becca first suffered the warning seizure, we were determined to make the journey as positive as we could. This challenge has not proved as difficult as we imagined, for out of all the sorrow have shone the most amazing examples of humanity. The human spirit has been revealed at its most brilliant.

We are so proud of our daughter. Against all the odds she has continued to fight – no matter what cruelty melanoma threw at her. She had the most amazing capacity to remain focused on survival and if sheer willpower had been enough then she would surely have conquered her cancer. As it was she defied her medical team and out lived the predicted 'few months'! It was a hard route to follow and a demanding life style which she adopted and yet, through all this, she remained ever-concerned for those around her, ever able to make us laugh – and we feel privileged to have shared her journey and witnessed her amazing courage and strength.

And every beat of this journey has been shared by her partner Kev. Kevin Sinton B.A. (Fine Art) had just graduated when Becca first became ill. He immediately became her 'carer' and for two years he has been her constant support – surrounding her with love – being her provider, her guide, and her inspiration. We are so grateful that he has been there for all of us –calm, caring and strong. A wonderful person.

And when we asked for help there appeared hundreds of 'angels' who showered us with love, prayers (of all dimentions) and money. Without this financial help it would have proved very difficult to maintain Becca's fight. She tried so very hard, along a pathway which she felt offered her the best chance of survival. You gave her hope. You are all such lovely people.

There will be a private family cremation and Bec's ashes will be scattered around her favourite place on the edge of Bodmin Moor. We would ask that each one of you just takes a few moments to reflect on the wonder of her life – and do whatever you feel appropriate. Listen to a piece of music, light a candle, and if you are part of the Middlesex University crowd – have a Jack Daniels.

Peter Kaye 30th May 2007

Becca's 'send off' was as theatrical as we could make it. We worked hard to avoid the sentiment as Becca had instructed. Elvis featured, together with Neil

Diamond and "The Sound of Music" – with a bit of jiving and lots of sunflowers and bright colours. It was not easy but we performed with a degree of flair worthy of a true BAPA (B.A. Performance Arts)

Several of us wrote poetry :

It happens but once in a Lifetime
Smooth, silken moment fluttering
my heart like the humming bird's wing
awakening my soul from its cold lonely dream.
You gave me your kingdom
your love, soul and heart
you showed me the lotus afloat in my dark
you were my Buddha
my Christ
my Krishna
my life
my lover
my friend
my soul and my light.
Snug within the warm womb of love and intimacy
we ran and laughed like soft, mad,
euphoric children within a new
velvet wonderland.
Yet cruel, wretched fate has torn
our dreams
our future
our purpose
our place
we've lost for this lifetime
that which I'll never replace

yet know that we tasted a deep pure true love
and swam in the comfort of our bliss, lust and trust.
Ride the plains my sweet one
my Tatanka
one day we'll run again
free
no boundaries
no pain
together
at peace
I love you
forever.
Kevin Sinton 5ᵗʰ June 2007

Becca
The theatre is empty now
By day, the sunlight slants
On battered boards.
By night, the moonlight
Milks the mute applause
Of silent rows.
Whatever play was here
Has now moved on.
The curtains closed,
And audiences, stirred,
Have now to homes all gone.
But through these doors,
In rivers of bright voices,
Rushing on through valleyed woods
And tumbling down towards the sea,
The story of the world still courses,

Told – as it must always be –
From the moment it is lived
Until the oceans set it free.
Francis Hallam 5th June 2007

Just what did those 'Daily Mail' readers miss!

Monday 15th February 2016

Today I have just completed this previous section 'The Daily Mail' and for reasons which may be obvious to you I have found this so difficult to write. A fortnight ago I stopped writing. I know why. The glass of wine in Joan's garden and the 'Daily Mail' would lead me to dealing with Becca's fight for survival – and her ultimate death.

I took a break and drove up last week to Exeter to stay a couple of nights with Fran and Jennie. I took my opening chapters with me for them to read. I trust their opinion although I appreciate that they are far too close to be unbiased. They were unequivocal in their belief that I should continue. As hard as it would be I had to deal with what was the most tragic and traumatic event that Bet and I would ever have to face.

I have written the last pages through tears and I have discovered that which I suspected. Bet faced so much of this alone. I was caught up in a whirlwind of organisation and I protected myself. I thought that we shared our grief – but perhaps sorrow which is so deep is impossible to share. Each one of us has to work through it in our own way. As I now read Bet's diaries for the first time I am only just beginning to grasp her frailty and her need for more support.

It's a bit of a concern to me, the flippancy of my verses, but I am not sure if I can open my heart about my mother – Becca relationship. Am I hiding behind denial or am I so shallow it's not there – or is it just that it was so hugely my life that I don't need to explain it or 'out' it? She was my daughter, my first 'go' at motherhood. We were soul mates in our understandings of the world and of our spirituality. We laughed a lot, we had secrets, we loved plants and the relationship between them in the garden, the birth of lovely flowers and vegetables from seeds – this is so inadequate! I can't say what our joint bodies meant to each other – so the verse about 'coffee enemas' will suffice
Bet Kaye 3rd June 2007

Forgive me Bet. I thought you were the strong one. Perhaps you always were.

On my journey back from Exeter the memories were conjured yet again by all those familiar pieces of landscape. The only difference is that on the tree-lined hill before Launceston the landscape has changed. High behind the trees is the silhouette of a giant wind turbine. Great! I called to visit Kev. He has a lovely little flat out in the wilds – part of the delightfully named Old Wit Farm. It is bounteous in its supply of memories – for pieces of Becca's life adorn the walls and shelves. And Becca's cat Millie (who must be 18 at least) greets me like an old friend.

Kev still grieves for Becca – although he now

works in a local care home and has begun to paint again in bright colours. He produces a notebook – of Becca's. In it there are her scribbled thoughts written at various times throughout her illness. I will include a couple of extracts here:

Night of Change 27th August 2006 …
I'm tired. Tired of being scared. I am so tired of this. I know though that this is my life and I should enjoy it – but I am so tired. I don't know how to do this. It should be possible – but how? I want life – but I don't want to fuck it up and I feel as though I am fucking it up in all that I feel and do. I want to be positive. I want to survive. I want to be a survivor – not just a fighter. I think this is the first time that I have really had to face this – that there is no help from anywhere else. It is up to me, to my body and brain but they are so tired. Everyone around me is so fantastic but I feel I am letting them down. I will die and I will let them down. My life will be gone and I so want my life. It's so brilliant. It can be such a fantastic life but it has to be without the cancer. I want to get rid of all the cancer from my body but to do that I have to change and to embrace my life as it is …
… I have always felt that there was a purpose for life. There must be more than a strangled, fearful, stressed, anxiety-ridden life without hope or purpose. Whoever is out there please help me find my positive, fighting, hopeful, purposeful life – and please help me to sleep .. I need to sleep .. to heal myself.
Becca Kaye 27th August 2006

*I hate this. I feel there is no time left. I feel as though
I have failed. I am scared. I am so sad. I want to be
happy. I want a life again but I am fucked up. I just
cry. I love everyone so much. I feel as though I am
letting them down – or maybe they would be better
off without me? I want to be me without cancer. I
want to laugh and dance and sing. My brain hurts.
I want to be better soon. There are so many wankers
in this world – so many people without any idea who
are fucking up the planet. I am a good one. Surely I
deserve the chance of life? I feel as though I have been
hit again. I don't know how to get up. Help me! This is
a loop. How the fuck do I get out of it?*
Becca Kaye April 2007

I promised some positives.

The positive has to be that Becca lived her short life
to the full. She made so many people laugh (and cry),
and her vivacity and joy for living will remain in the
hearts of all who knew her.

Now perhaps I can continue to write this book!

"Pete's holding a purple knife!"

Wednesday 30th September 2015

Such a jungle of emotions! I've never 'done drugs' but the kaleidoscopic induced heights must be paled by how I am feeling now as I enter Kenwyn. The foyer is luxuriously palatial and Ross's smile from behind the reception desk is reassuring. Bet must be still be with me. I have been away, on my own, for the past few days and in some ways I feel different. For the first couple of days my thoughts were constantly about Bet but, little by little, I feel that I have been able to reclaim something of myself. I had spent the best part of my return journey talking to my railway companions and there were fractions of my mind which now felt rejuvenated in some way. There was the inevitable feeling of guilt and that was soon to surface with a vengeance.

Bet is, today, in her wheelchair by the window, awkwardly slumped, and she manages a contorted smile of recognition. The offer of goodies from the cool bag is accepted and we slip easily into our new routine. I ask about her visitors over the past few days but she shows little recognition. She remembers, when prompted, that Mary came one day, and Ann and Kevin on another afternoon – but it seems that Sue and Ian B didn't make the trip. I feel disappointed – but Bet doesn't seem to mind. Strange really –

especially as Ian B can figure so much in her fantasy world. I talk to her about my visit to the Isle of Wight and begin to show her the photos I took of my journey. I begin with a shot of the train pulling into Platform 3 at Truro – a place where so many of our adventures had begun. Bet's reaction is difficult to read – but then I have found that an impossible task for the past two years. She is not interested. I sense a sadness – possibly regret. I change my plans. To share this journey is not perhaps so wise. Have I made Bet unhappy? Now the guilt really does begin to choke me and I fight back the tears. I produce the stones I have brought her back from the island – and talk about the special ones selected by Joan and Peter. There is just enough acknowledgement to make me feel that it is worth continuing, but Bet seems tired – or aggrieved – or annoyed – or just plain bored by my pathetic prattling and by me. The constant limbo of the carer's role; the drip gradually eroding any confidence. Now I feel guilty again. How could I feel sorry for myself when Bet is in her real nightmare – enchained by a body that no longer does anything that she must yearn to do?

How guilty I now feel about my reactions when, two years ago, it became obvious that Bet's reality was no longer mine. The images of Christmas 2013 with our verbal battles over dangerously excessive use of culinary herbs; of friends 'dying' and their partners creating romantic relationships with Bet in her new found freedom; with a perplexing demand for love-making (she hated it if I ever referred to 'sex') several times each day whilst a growing distance seemed to be opening between us. One sign of Frontotemporal Dementia, which I was later to discover, is that beliefs become obsessions – and this was certainly the case with Bet. Her belief that herbs would cure her ocular herpes meant that we were visiting the Health Food shop every day – where she would produce the carefully folded plastic bags to be refilled from the apothecary jars. Her religious addiction to pepper and its synergistic properties meant that the stuff was flung copiously over everything on the table. Her belief that acidophilus was an aid to helping avoid constipation led to a particularly difficult situation. I realised that she was opening up to ten capsules each morning and pouring the contents onto her bowl of fruit. I would try reasoning – but would get nowhere. I would question her logic and the result would be anger and distress. She would accuse me of being determined to prolong her problems and of wanting her to 'go blind' – for whenever she became upset she claimed that her herpes would flair up. She could have been right of course. My behaviour, at times angry, was hardly helpful and she saw through my attempts to curb her excesses. I would ask her to limit the acidophilus and place two capsules by her fruit bowl. She agreed, and for a few days I thought that my negotiations had been successful. Then I realised that the 'new' jar, which at the beginning of the week had contained 120 capsules, was now empty. She was secretly taking more and 'hiding' the evidence – throwing the broken capsule shells into the waste bin. I remember being very upset that my trust seemed to count for so little – and I now realise that Bet was feeling so badly let down by my behaviour. We were both in a chaotic world where our ability to communicate had discontinued. Our relationship seemed to have been severed. Bet had always kept a diary and until it became obvious what was happening and that she had a recognisable form of dementia I did not read it. I respected her privacy. During January 2014 I had also kept some notes. I had taken Bet to visit our GP and we were awaiting some form of mental assessment. I thought it might be useful to have a record of what was happening. To juxtapose our contrasting reactions throws some interesting and disturbing reflections.

> *Please Guardian Angel come and get me – make me better... I have to say it is all a bit stressy here... someone has no sense of humour. I wish my leg would get better. I wish you would come. I need so much help...*
> *Bet Kaye 2nd January 2014*

And so the diary shares Bet's fears regarding the increased difficulty with walking – but with me there would be the constant denial that anything was wrong. Several times each day she would make reference to the fact that on Christmas Day I had suggested that she took an 'acyclovir' tablet to subdue a very angry eye. Her programme of herbs had been designed to avoid ever having to take acyclovir ever again.

*Big row over the acyclovir incident. He won't agree
that he made me take it. I know he insisted – for me
that's the end of the story – but he's made a list of his
version ..*
Bet Kaye 7th January 2014

In my anxious state I was still trying to bring some logic
to bear. This wouldn't be the last time that I was to resort
to writing down the sequence of events in an attempt to
justify my actions. And it wouldn't be the last time that
I was to find my notes torn to shreds and littered in a
basket. Sam too would try to reason with her mum.

*Sam popped in. Always lovely to see her. She thinks
Pete's criticism of my obsessions is because he cares....
But my response is – if he cares why does he go on
about it? He knows the worry will make my eye red
again.*
Bet Kaye 13th January 2014

Catch 22 yet again! I defended myself but there was
no understanding of my frustration. Similarly it was
obvious that Bet was also confused and distressed
with the way that I was behaving. Two days later we
were to meet up with good friends Dave and Angie
from Bodmin. We met for lunch at a rather crowded
local restaurant. The journey there had been angry
because I had forgotten to put a bottle of water in the
car. Bet was now becoming obsessional about water
consumption and had in her mind that at least three
litres each day was essential. By the end of this year

this particular obsession was to lead her into a coma and close to death – but for now it was merely another need that I was expected to fuel. The bar was very busy but Bet demanded that I got her an apple juice. She wouldn't wait just a few minutes for our friends to arrive. I must have shown a degree of frustration when Dave and Angie came in …

> *I didn't realise that Pete would tell our great friends that I was losing it! (Alzheimer's perhaps) Maybe he thinks that is so. How could he undermine me like this? We've been married now for 45 years and he is still saying I am losing it! Why the hell did he marry me if he is going to undermine me in this way? Everything bloody does! Sam realised many years ago there would be someone else and hoped that there would be. When I have thoughts sometimes it happens and I think we have finally got to a point when we'll get together. I can't believe this person has been with me forever – and now I know that life has brought us together at this late stage in our lives. He even visited Angie and told her that he could do this for me. I never knew even this guardian angel might do this for me. I think the time has come. What a rant! The meal was lovely! Bet Kaye 15th January 2014*

I certainly would never have suggested 'Alzheimers' but obviously my anger had been evident to Bet. Angie and Dave were to note how strange Bet was behaving. She ordered a risotto and laced it with sauces. My notes mention how mustard was poured over. There was never enough moisture with any meal. Basic table manners were gradually disappearing and allowing her to be alone in the kitchen was becoming potentially dangerous. That evening I discovered a brew of herbs burned black on the stove. Such an event inevitably led us into argument. I had yet to learn that logic could be totally missing in Bet's new mind. She would claim time after time that acidophilus not only would have aided her bowel movements but it would have helped to cure her eye. The tautological lament continued and now she adds that her eye was better before we had gone to Sicily. To go there had been my idea. She had not wanted to go. How I am ashamed of myself as I look back to such occasions – for I would become angry, raise my voice and swear! No wonder she began to see me in such a miserable light.

From this point onwards Bet's diary becomes increasingly distressing for me to read – never mind understand. There is daily reference to 'liebe' – sometimes as often as three sessions. I remember these times vividly of course. Bet was insatiable – but alarmingly so. I was being assessed for possible prostate problems, reassuring myself that the raised PSA level of 30+ was nothing to worry about. I was having to wee very frequently – especially during the night and I was shattered. Bet seemed to have become selfish and totally focussed on physical sex – of all shapes and manoeuvres. Her diaries refer to my sleepless nights and my visits to the doctor but there is no sense that her behaviour is adding to my problems. Her doubts about my faithfulness reached an alarming crescendo.

I had a text today from Ann to say that Pete's had sex with her five times in the last years since we first met them. What was he thinking about? Does he think that I don't care about him sleeping with other people? Finished! I've never slept with ANY ONE ELSE AT ALL. HAD CHANCES BUT NEVER TAKEN THEM – HE EVEN MADE ME TAKE ACYCLOVIR WHICH MADE MY EYE RED. Watched the new Three Musketeers and really enjoyed it...
Bet Kaye 19th January 2014

My own notes show how her feelings were manifest in her actions.

Bet was very tense from awakening. There was a frenetic session of 'physical sex' which she demanded. Her face never relaxed throughout. Her body was tense. She needed to know if I had been faithful to her but I couldn't reassure her. She seemed no longer to have any trust in me. She mentioned that Ann had made me a nice cake – and appeared jealous. She complained of indigestion. Acidophilus would help. She would press points. (always very much into reflexology). Period of repetition and when I tried to reassure her she terminated the conversation and disappeared to do yoga. She did not do any yoga (finding it increasingly difficult) but spent time talking to herself...
Peter Kaye 19th January 2014

Both Bet and myself were facing a barrage of medical tests as a diagnosis, for both of us, as our very caring

GP was very thorough and she began to eliminate possible causes for Bet's increasing physical and mental problems. There was no sign of a stroke and Bet's thyroid only needed a little attention.

Pretty good liebe ... set off to Trago (a local store) *but came back as I needed the loo... pity I have a bit of pain but I keep my legs out straight. It seems Pete has been making love to a few ladies and men. I wonder what he thinks is missing from our relationship ... Saw the doctor today and am to have an MRI scan. Have I really got Alzheimer's? Pete seems to think that I get terribly confused ...*
Bet Kaye 21st January 2014

Rampant and demanding sex. She seemed disappointed with my 'performance' and many questions again about my loyalty. We set off to Trago but she came back. I suspect her leg is causing her concern. Dr called us in for test results. Bet didn't want to go. Just wanted to phone for results. Didn't want me to go into the surgery with her. Got very angry with me. Seems there is a problem with the head scan. Now perhaps an MRI scan and a referral to a geriatric specialist. Bet must hate this. She was very unhappy about the fact that I mentioned her 'confusion' – although she did accept that she hears voices. She also cried when we talked about Becca. This all seems fine – but how long have we to wait before I can know what is happening?
Peter Kaye 21st January 2014

The 'rampant sex' and the doubt about my faithfulness are obviously linked. She seemed to be fighting to keep my attention. If only she had known how devoted I was to her. Perhaps if I had spent more time reassuring her instead of allowing my frustration and anger to show, then some of the stress could have been alleviated? I did, often, tell her that she was wrong to doubt me but perhaps someone in the earlier stages of dementia needs far more support?. Our Kev did tell me that I should go along with whatever Bet says. He suggested that I should not try to argue but should agree with whatever Bet would say. It did help a little but it was impossible for me to agree that I had been unfaithful. It was increasing hard to continue to watch as Bet began to drink more and more prune juice as yet another activity became obsessional.

The 'prune juice' period caused me a few blushes. I was later to realise that these 'obsessions' would pass – and be replaced. At the time, however, there was no insight into how long each would last. The thought that every day I would have to go down into town and buy at least four bottles of prune juice filled me with dread. I emptied the shelves at Holland and Barrett – but the staff there understood. They knew us both well and I had felt able to explain how Bet was now behaving. Their limited stock was gone within a few days but thankfully I discovered that Tesco carried a supply discreetly positioned on a top shelf. I tried, whenever possible, to use the self-service check-out but even there I felt that eyes were on me as the bottles clanked dully into my bags. Stupidly I could rarely refrain from some form of sarcastic comment as I begrudgingly unloaded the daily ration. As I reflect back I wish that I had been able to just accept this, along with all the other demands which were to follow, and that this was Bet's new reality. It was, in her mind, an essential need, and I really ought to have just accepted it without question. Bet certainly was becoming increasingly annoyed with what she saw as my unnecessary interference.

> *He's still writing down my evacuation times and had limited my prune juice. Who am I to be treated like this? Since we went to Tregoad (Nov 13) it has been like this. I fight back – but hey ho!*
> *Bet Kaye 22nd January 2014*

The following day we walked over to Ann and Kevin's for an evening meal. Bet was obviously finding walking increasingly difficult.

> *Quite a walk! It seems longer each time. We spent some time in the study before a pleasant simple veggie casserole followed by blackcurrant meringue. We enjoyed time in the sitting room with a lovely log fire. It was very nice sitting there with a whisky with Kevin...*
> *Bet Kaye 23rd January 2014*

My notes for the same day refer to Bet's confused state of mind. So many times she would ask if and when we were going out. During our evening with our friends she had been fairly relaxed and contributed quite sensibly to most of the conversation. I did note, however, that there was much 'false' laughter, totally out of character, and often in inappropriate places. Once again though, following time we would spend with our friends, jealousy, again so out of character, was to raise doubts in Bet's mind.

> *Thought we both enjoyed love-making, but tonight I wonder if Pete loves me enough. Seems he has fallen head over heels in love with her! More intellectual I imagine!! ...I wish I hadn't been made to take acyclovir... I could write before my brain was taken away... written strange things. I've never done this. It has usually been less personal...*
> *Bet Kaye 25th January 2014*

The following morning Bet's diary entry describes the fact that her mind 'is all over the place' and she found that she could not sleep. I was later to discover that she had sent Sue a very strange 'text' in the middle of the night.

At this time Bet was still attempting to follow her habit of a twenty minute session of yoga each morning – something she had done for the past couple of years. I wonder if it was related to her realisation that all was no longer right with her body – all part of the 'healthy life-style' together with the herbal remedies, the organic diet and the drive to drink enough water (filtered of course!). It was becoming obvious that some of this physical routine was no longer possible

– not that she ever expressed any concern to me. This was her 'private' life and something which she didn't share. Sometimes I could hear her talking to herself – or perhaps it was to Becca.

I had made a conscious effort to share her recent love of jigsaw puzzles. This too was now becoming an obsession. She had initially been completing them at the rate of two each week and we were well known now in the charity shops. We particularly liked puzzles from The Cornwall Hospice shop – for there we were guaranteed that all puzzles sold would be complete. Apparently they had two volunteers who checked each puzzle. There was a job we could easily have done! I think I started to help when Bet was beginning to find it difficult, sometimes struggling with the same piece to furiously make it fit somewhere. Was this her way of trying to sort out the growing puzzles in her mind? These were usually quiet times. There were no arguments around the dining table when the puzzles were out, and she seemed more relaxed. Conversation would pass for 'normal'. I yearned for such times for I was never able to predict how Bet would react to anything I said. I wrote down a typical conversation on the afternoon of 27th January

Bet   *I need another bottle of ginko.* (she was taking tincture of Ginko as an aid to memory)

Pete   *Oo! That's the second in two weeks.*

Bet   *Well! I'm only taking a normal dose every night!*

Pete   *You must be taking more than that. One bottle normally lasts you a month.*

Bet	*I'm only taking the normal dose.*
Pete	*Impossible. Are you maybe forgetting?*
Bet	*(angrily) If you don't get me more ginko then I will have to have more prune juice!*
Pete	*(getting frustrated) Why?*
Bet	*For constipation! Why else! You made me take the acyclovir! What do you care! And you stopped me having acidophilus! Are you stopping me having everything?*
Pete	*Of course not. I just don't want you taking too many. You know that taking 120 acydophilus tablets in one week wasn't wise.*
Bet	*(now shouting and very distressed) Why are you counting!? Were you counting?*
Pete	*Yes I was. Why did you pretend to be having two each day when you were secretly taking at least ten?*
Bet	*It was to stop my bottom bleeding! I needed to stop my bottom bleeding!*
Pete	*So what is happening now?*
Bet	*My bottom is always bleeding! And it is your fault!*
Pete	*Oh no! So without acidophilus you will bleed to death?*
Bet	*You want me to die! Then you can marry someone else!*
Pete	*You know that's not true!*
Bet	*(screaming through tears) You do want me to die!*

How I squirm now as I reflect back on such conversations over which I seemed to have no control. At this stage I was still trying to bring some logic back into Bet's life. I had no idea as to how to deal with such situations. Later I became far more tolerant and I learned not to argue or be critical, but now I was blundering in a frightening unknown and probably doing far too much harm. To what extent was I compounding Bet's fears and undermining her confidence even further? It seems to be a well-known fact that dementia sufferers will be angry towards their 'nearest and dearest'? Is this because they see and hear their partner behaving strangely and often angrily towards them? They will see nothing wrong with their own behaviour. Their new world is their new reality. And in this world they are witnessing unthinking and sometimes disturbing reactions from those closest to them. Just as I was frustrated and saddened by Bet's behaviour – she must have been equally distressed. Her partner, her best friend for over fifty years, was now no longer easy going and smiling. He was frowning, distrusting and sometimes possibly frightening in his reactions. We were both now in worlds where we could no longer trust each other. We were unable to communicate as our realities had totally drifted apart.

Over the next few weeks Bet's diary entries reflect growing tension between us. She would constantly accuse me of spying and wanting her to be blind or lame; there would be repetition of the fact that I was being unfaithful; nothing I did was as she wanted it; and the loop of prune juice, acyclovir and acidophilus became an almost constant. I did occasionally crack. There can be no excuse and I wish that I had never become angry.

I'm not sure what happened. We were both shouting. He called me a 'sarcastic cow'! It was dreadful. They were words that never should have been said. Finally there were tears and everything was OK...
Bet Kaye 1st February 2014

I seem to have annoyed Pete re his adultery. I really don't mind...
Bet Kaye 2nd February 2014

We have had a very happy relationship. He thinks I am having an affair with Ian B – but I've NEVER HAD AN AFFAIR WITH ANYBODY...
Bet Kaye 3rd February 2014

At some point I think Pete's been confronted by his sexual past and problems thus caused and attitudes changed...
Bet Kaye 5th February 2014

Would love to be able to walk faster. It just takes me ages. Can't believe that P (the surgeon who operated on Bet's arm) *and what he did to me. Don't suppose he'll ever be sacked...*
We had a lovely meal at The Thai Orchid this evening...
Bet Kaye 6th February 2014

This was the evening that we had joined Sue and Ian B for a meal before they were to set off on their travels. It had been quite a difficult day where Bet had constantly had to be reminded that we were dining out. Her short-term memory was becoming a problem and within minutes it seems that she had forgotten that were going out. During the meal her conversation never seemed to link with what everyone else was saying. When Bet went off to the toilet Ian B told us that she had been fondling his leg under the table throughout the meal. On our walk home through town her loud conversation was about making love!

Over the next days she seemed to be forgetting more and becoming more confused. She could never find her special things and accused me of hiding them. She now wanted to take her lip balm, her glasses and her jacket everywhere with her. They were never where she left them and she felt that I was deliberately hiding them. It seemed obvious to her that I wanted her to think that she was 'going mad'. Not content with trying to make her blind and restricting everything she held dear, I was now trying to get her 'sectioned'! My notes detail that she would take our house key out with her into the garden to stop me locking her out. I now would try to joke about the fact that her things would disappear and sometimes she would join in with this laughter. It was extreme laughter – and sounded forced – but it was so much better than the anger and violence that was now becoming the norm, She would sit clutching her bag where she has stowed her lip balm and hand cream. As soon as she put it down it seemed to disappear. She was adamant that it has moved! And that I had maliciously moved it!

She slipped out of the car one morning in town whilst I was parking. She told me that she would just pop to the health food shop and be back in five minutes. I waited fifteen minutes but there was no sign of her. I ran up High Street. Yes she had been to the shop for they remembered her well. Where had she gone? I searched the streets. There was no sign. I drove home but she was not there. Just as I was thinking that I would have to contact the police I got a call from our friend Maggie. Bet was with her and in rather a confused state as she didn't know where I was. She seemed glad to see me but was totally oblivious to the anxiety she had caused. Only now, as I look back, do I realise that my own health was in a pretty fragile state. I was having to fit in my own blood tests, heart monitors and visits to urology. Only later was urology to be replaced by oncology! I feel a song coming on! No way thankfully did I have the time or energy to feel worried by my own situation. In fact any enforced trip to my GP (who always gave me such a welcome hug!), or to hospital, was a refreshing break!

We were, however, reaching crisis point. She began to send out texts to Ian B at 10.30 in the evening whist I was having a bath. She asked him to meet her.

We've had a few 'does' today but I hope tomorrow will be the right time. Don't really know if Ian B's coming

As I now look at her distorted body, which appears so uncomfortable in her wheel chair, I find it hard to equate this scene with February 2014. I complete the afternoon's routine with a brush of the teeth and a swill of the mouthwash. As we have the wheel chair I suggest a trip down the corridor to the far lounge. It is quiet today as the man who constantly shouts seems to have been moved into a far wing. We pass rooms where the inhabitants look out at us. I always smile and greet them. There is often a sense that they are lonely and would love more conversation. My Bet – the old Bet – would have been in her element – especially as many of the residents here do not suffer from dementia and would love more friendship. The staff here are caring and hard working but there is never enough time and the bells are always calling. The activities team run quite a full programme. On our second day here we had been into the lounge to meet some owls from the Owl Sanctuary. The following day I wheeled Bet to the lounge where we had 'songs from the sixties' – something Bet would have relished a few months before. Now, however, she had asked to return to her room after half an hour. There is so much here that Bet would have loved but her horizons are now so limited.

We reach the far lounge with its panoramic view over the city. I point out the cathedral and the railway station down in the valley. I then notice a rabbit munching away under the hedge. Bet is animated once again and talks of her childhood. Our conversation is lucid and meaningful. Is it really possible that last year she had thought that I was about to kill her?

I left home last night and ran up to Sam's. I had seen Pete holding a purple knife. He was going to kill me Bet Kaye 15th February 2014

"Just a tickle of psychiatric drugs!"

Wednesday 7th October 2015

Bet's sitting in her wheelchair by the window. Recently she has sometimes said that she has felt cold so today I have brought her a small shawl. The cheerful carer assures me that she has had a good lunch. There is evidence of food spilled down her blouse but I doubt if she has eaten much. I sense that the staff here think that I will feel less anxious if they assure me that she is 'getting better'. That will never be. I know that. Every day now she is a little weaker. It can only be a question of time. As I sit on her bed wet, through with sweat – cursing the hot flushes which are a distracting and sometimes even welcome side-effect of my hormone injections, she is anxious to discover the delights in the cool bag which I have dragged once again up the hill. This visit is such a pleasure after the last two years. She isn't shouting at me. There are no looks of hatred. I have wanted to look after Bet, to comfort her and reassure her that I would always be by her side. That has been impossible of course for her illness has divided us and torn us apart. Forget the heroic glow – caring has been a battle!

The day when Bet first ran away from home in fear of the purple knife was Friday 14th February 2014 – Valentine's Day. It also happened to be a full moon – a point that Bet noted in her diary. The writing that day reveals nothing of the torturous feelings which must have been flooding her mind. She talks fondly of spending time in the garden preparing bags in which she would grow the new potatoes which we both loved. There is no mention of the fact that she took the door key out with her – afraid that I would lock her out. She seems almost ecstatic over the Valentine's meal that I cooked for her. The M & S special deal is praised at least twice with a ravenous mention going to 'ginger chocolates'. The same Bet of course who, four months previously, had ranted about our diet of excessive sugar.

For some reason we were a little late setting off for bed. We followed the same routine every night – for Bet enjoyed a bath rather than a shower. And so, ever conscious of saving water, we would share a bath. I would go first as Bet preferred the water to be cooler. I dried myself and shouted down to her that the bath was ready. There was silence. She had gone. I grabbed my clothes and dashed out into the roadway. Almost midnight and I was running from street to street – shoes but no socks, jeans but no pants, and a flimsy T-shirt! And I didn't pick up my mobile – otherwise my nightmare would have been curtailed. As it was I spent a good half an hour running to junctions and just hoping that I would catch sight of her – or find her sitting on a wall. This is the stuff of real nightmares. When I returned home there was a message on the answer phone. It was from Sam to say that her mum had arrived at their house, battered on the door to awaken them, and was claiming that I was going to kill her. She had explained that she had hidden the knives in the garden because a neighbour had told her that she was going to be 'sectioned'. She did say to Sam, however, that she did wonder if she was imagining these things.

"Maybe I am going mad? He tells me I am going mad!" she confided to Sam.

Ian drove her back home in the early hours of Saturday morning. She seemed calm and so he left. I ran her another bath but then she refused to come into bed. She claimed that she needed to finish writing a letter to her cousin Frances and went down stairs. I began to write up my own notes of the night's events. I had just written, "I should perhaps have double-locked the door" when I heard an ominous slam. Bet had gone. I grabbed some clothing yet again – but by the time I had got out onto the road there was no sign. Just streetlights and the glow of the harbour below. She made it safely back to Sam's house – maybe half a mile at the most – wearing just the T-shirt in which she usually slept. This time she stayed there.

It seems that it is always the weekend when I need urgent medical help. How I wished that I could just talk to my lovely GP. The 'out-of – hours' service was understanding and offered a prescription, something with a low dose, which I could administer if Bet felt threatened again. Ian brought her home again. She was wearing some of Sam's clothes and looked pale and unhappy. We all sat together and Bet told me about her dream and how she had hidden the knives in a water butt in the garden. She still couldn't remember where she had hidden the door key. I tried to keep the day as calm as possible but over an early supper she seemed to 'flip' and accused me again of not caring about her eye, her arm or her hand. Despite my best efforts I fear there was a degree of indignation in my response and Bet retaliated by telling me that she felt like running away again. Apparently, she continued, Sam had telephoned someone who would help but I had cancelled it. Later, when Sam telephoned, I asked Sam to explain to her mum that this had not happened. No use! After the call Bet was still insistent that Sam had made 'special arrangements' and that I would not allow treatment to be given.

After supper we went down to The Poly and watched a play. It was quite thought provoking and we discussed it in detail as we walked home hand in hand. We managed to joke about 'running away' and we discussed that there was a 'problem' and that we would 'sort it together'. Bet had her tot of whisky and a ginger chocolate. All seemed fine. I thought that I had managed to bring back my Bet.

I awoke with a start. The telephone was ringing. It was 4am. Sam's voice calmly told me not to worry. Mum was safely with them. I reached over to the other side of the bed. It was empty! Bet stayed at Sam's house over the Sunday until we were able to get medical help on Monday morning. Oh for a 24/7 Health Service!

On that Sunday I had time to myself and to put down some thoughts onto paper. I felt that these would be necessary to help the medical team make decisions. It was obvious that we all needed help. My research over the past month had discovered that in 10% of people with Motor Neurone Disease there is an associated form of dementia – Frontotemporal Dementia (sometimes abbreviated as FTD). I listed the symptoms and noted the similarity. I was convinced that this was the cause of Bet's wild behaviour but I tried to present a balanced view:

Notes re Mrs Betty Kaye

Frontotemporal dementia?

Inappropriate behaviour in public *
Impulsivity *
Loss of inhibitions *
Overeating, a change in food preferences, poor table manners *
Neglect of personal hygiene
Repetitive or obsessional behaviour *
Seemingly more selfish *
Inability to empathise with others – cold and uncaring *
Irritability *
Tactless or rude
More or less outgoing
Lethargic. Lacking enthusiasm
Depression *   * Relevant to Bet's behaviour*

Or is this Emotional breakdown as a result of:

Herpes in eye – for 12 years Bet has fought to rid herself of this and having to use Acyclovir. This is a constant battle and a large part of her daily routine

Five years ago Becca (elder daughter) died at the age of 35 of metastatic melanoma – having fought for two years using diet and natural therapy (the NHS gave her two months to live)

Three years ago Bet fell several times off a bicycle, which she felt damaged her shoulder. Her arm muscles wasted and a year ago an operation took place to repair the nerves. This also involved wrist work. After the operation Bet has had no use of thumb and forefinger – as a result has lost the ability to play the piano, to sew, to prepare food, even gardening – all the things she loved. She is distressed by the fact that she has to rely on me to help her with everyday tasks. This problem has recently been diagnosed as Monomelic amyotrophy and she has been referred to MND coordinator. This Bet did not accept.

A couple of months ago her left leg has developed a muscular problem and produced a clumpy walk which has slowed her down considerably. She does have spasms in both legs. Again Bet is convinced that this is the direct result of a slip at the bottom of our garden steps.

It may be – but it does appear that MND could be happening. Perhaps the initial lack of balance on the bike, the arm, the leg and the dementia are all part of the same picture. If this is so then we need an accurate diagnosis – and there are planning implications.

The mental problems are now of serious concern. Bet is now convinced that I intend to kill her. She hid my kitchen knives in a water butt in the garden. She leaves the house during the night and 'escapes' up to our daughter Sam's house. She also feels that I am attempting to make her blind – and am not interested in helping to make her leg / arm better. I limit her natural therapies and she also claims that I monitor and restrict her freedom. She takes the door key with her when she goes in the garden in case I lock her out (she hides these and can't remember where)

There are cases both Sam and I have tried to reason with her to perhaps limit the 'natural therapies' she takes. For example she is consumed by the fear of constipation and daily slurps vast quantities of slippery elm and prune juice etc. She was also taking about 10 high strength acidophilus tablets a day (going to great lengths to show me that she was only taking three). We suggested that she stopped these – and she found that the lower stomach discomfort she had been feeling also stopped. This was why, even though she was having bowel movements 5/6 times a day, she was still convinced she had constipation. We keep a chart – but there is no way she will accept the logic. She still 'escaped' and bought more acidophilus tablets.

She is always thirsty and has dry lips, A lip balm has become her constant comfort companion which she uses every few minutes. Sometimes she becomes very angry – and cannot find it. It is never where she left it. I am accused of deliberately moving and hiding her things – trying to prove that she is mad. And the loop goes on again – her eye, her arm – I want her to go blind etc.etc.

Always eating. She tends to add throughout the meal. A lunchtime bowl of salad will then have

129

yoghurt poured on, pickle added, olives .... The fridge will be opened and another jar brought out. Salad cream dolloped! If we've been to the bakers she will have demanded a pie or a quiche ... a tin of fish ... plus some chicken slices... Breakfast is a similar concoction with the contents of several natural therapies poured out (she doesn't like the gelatine capsule part!) She avoided wheat and sugar for the past year (to help her eye) but now seems to be eating chocolate etc... Now taken to a glass of whisky every night.

Bet has always had a 'healthy sex drive' and enjoyed the physical side. However for the past two months this has become increasingly demanding. There are no inhibitions. She constantly tells me that she loves me and that she has always been faithful. At times she has angrily suggested that I think she is having an affair. Her diary refers to the fact that a friend of ours (IB) will soon be picking her up and taking her away. IB has recently left the country and Bet sat next to him at a farewell meal – during which she frequently rubbed his leg under the table. Bet often says that his partner has died. She claims that she has received texts or that she has 'heard voices'. I know IB well and there is no way he has encouraged Bet. The voices lead her to strange situations. I once returned home (in the early stages) to find several carrier bags containing towels. These were for Sam who was just about to pick them up. Sam was in Oxford and didn't want towels.

Bet is no longer the caring, sensitive and warm person she was. There are times when one could almost believe that she was her old self.. but these are getting increasingly rare. It is a knife-edge. Without keeping her on a lead I can no longer trust that she will stay with me. She 'forgets' where we are going – and why. I feel like her gaoler – and she sees me as that too. She is so frustrated and saddened by her situation. She is beginning to accept that she is confused and forgetting. She is sometimes genuinely saddened when she realises that her actions may have hurt someone – but more often is oblivious to their discomfort (especially mine!)

We all need help – and quickly. Peter Kaye 16th February 2014

Within an hour of phoning our GP a member of the Mental Health Team was sitting with Bet in Sam's lounge. I'll call her A – and she was to become a friend and tremendous support over the following year. She spent much time calmly talking with Bet – sometimes alone and then with either Sam or myself present. She explained to us all that she felt that a residential placement was necessary for assessment to take place – a place where Bet would feel safe and protected. She had 'Crossroads' in mind and would go back and hopefully arrange for a room to be made available. Bet's diary reveals that she had some understanding of the situation:

Went home to sort out tonight's tea which we got from M&S. We'd got chicken in the freezer so why we bought one I've no idea. Still you can always add great vegetables with it. Riverford will be here on

Wednesday so more vegetables will come. Did manage lovely liebe – always a joy. Feel as if my world is getting ever smaller. Did have an assessment earlier to find a place (safe) to stop my nightly ramblings. Things seem to be moving pretty fast. A popped round to assess this problem. She asked lots of basic questions for me to answer. Couldn't seem to think of four creatures beginning with 'S' – let's have a go! Shark, sheep, shearwater, squirrel, swift etc. So I am now off to an assessment centre funded by the NHS. Plans for drugs! Antipsychotic! Diazapan! Bit dire really. We ate at 7.30 and then headed up to Sam's where the evening was great. I felt a bit shivery so cuddled under a duvet …

Bet Kaye 17ᵗʰ February 2014

The following morning I collected Bet for the half hour drive to 'Crossroads' at Scorrier. Originally a motel it had recently been converted as a specialist residential home for people who suffered from dementia. Bet was expected and we were greeted with smiles. Those first few moments, when one enters a care home for the first time, are so important for all concerned and I felt a warm sense of comfort. I felt that I could trust these people to look after Bet with the care she deserved. Bet's room was spotlessly clean with a large window and en-suite bathroom. It was more like a hotel than the 'care home' image I had held in my mind and I am sure Bet felt the same relief. We were given a 'tour' and introduced to a motley crew of staff and clients. There were many smiles and Bet liked that. Staff met her with her name and had obviously been briefed. Most of the clients were elderly and it was obvious that Bet looked totally out of place as we were led by the twin tub washing machine and the aga, through to the tea shop and the bar, into a small lounge on several levels off which was a hair dressing salon, onwards into a larger room where dining tables were set for lunch and all around were comfortable settees. I noted a large basket full of fruit which was obviously available to anyone, and biscuits. There was a fish tank and lovely lighting. Music was playing in the large lounge – and it seemed comfortable and safe. Oh how I hoped that Bet would accept that this was a place where she would be cared for and made well again. But I had reservations. I left before lunch but knew I would be welcome back at any time of day or night. The staff made me feel good and I will always be grateful to them for that.

Arrived just before lunch and am now writing my diary.. I joined a table of very old ladies – they all seemed very old. Lunch was sausage and mash with peas, then fruit with clotted cream with a cuppa and some blackcurrant juice (ugh!) All very tasteless with no vegetables. I am truly bored. The old ladies couldn't empty the smallish plate. I feel like a prisoner in a place where there is no escape...
Bet Kaye 18th February 2014

I went in to visit the following morning and was distressed to find that all Bet's clothes had been packed. She had emptied her wardrobe and claimed that she wanted to go home. Apparently this happens as a matter of course with the vast majority of residents – and I was assured that she would settle in time. This wasn't how I saw things however. Bet was not here to become a resident in the sense that she was like the old ladies staring at the television or sitting silently in the corner. She was alive and her senses were alert. She must surely resent being here. I go in every day and take in the crossword and the suduko from the Daily 'I". Every day she is packed and ready to be taken home but seems to accept that her treatment here will eventually help her. By the end of the week it seems that she is more settled – although the staff do tell me that the previous evening she had stripped her room, packing as much as she could into her travel bag, and they had discovered her hatching an escape plan with an elderly resident. Apparently the pair of them were to sit on one of the sofas near to the door. When a member of staff released the lock to let a visitor in or out, then the old lady had to hurl her zimmer frame into the door way. Bet would then escape. The staff seemed to understand however and eventually Bet began to see herself as one of them.

They are such lovely people here and I feel so happy. There is such a nice variety of vegetables although I hope to get some watercress tomorrow. Dad is so good to me. It is a pity that he still has those knives ... fun with all the nurses and patients. It is good that I am able to heal people. That was lovely when they said

that they couldn't manage without me... It is good
to get exercise by walking round. There are flowers
everywhere – mostly artificial. I would love to get back
to my garden again...
Bet Kaye 21st February 2014

The staff had discovered that Bet felt that she could heal people. She did! Whilst we lived at Rylands she had begun to collect crystals and was fascinated by what she felt was their natural power. I remember when she began to help people – and there were many times when people brought their 'problems' and left with a lightened heart. A local man who had stuttered and stammered for years walked away able to chat at ease; allergies were sent packing, and a young boy with severe eczema came, held crystals, and his skin was clear within days. There were many others and Bet gave her time freely to help. I think she was able to offer them hope by listening and caring. She was just that kind of person. Now the staff at Scorrier also discovered that she loved flowers and placed her 'in charge' of floral arrangements. I was therefore to bring in daffodils from our friend Paul – the daffodil man. His bunches are so generous that for a few pounds Bet could fill the corridors with vibrant spring. I learned so much from observing the staff at 'Crossroads' – and it has remained the most effective and caring of all the homes into which I have been. They knew the clients so well and they entered their worlds – accepting their reality no matter how strange. I remember listening to a nurse talking with a 94 year old lady.

"Don't worry Gladys. All is in hand. The boat will leave here at 6pm just after tea. We will be landing in Redruth at 8pm and your mum and dad will be there to meet you. You'll have a lovely sail."

The old lady left smiling. Apparently this, or a similar conversation, will occur every afternoon – and Gladys remains content.

Such compassionate treatment is not without problems. Bet, in her new staff capacity as helper and healer, had decided that many of the 'poor old souls' didn't eat enough and she could no longer tolerate food being left on the plates. She was discovered 'force-feeding' several ladies who were obviously very distressed. Bet's responsibilities had to be limited. She felt a little aggrieved just as she did when they wouldn't allow her to have a key to the front door.

Not only was I learning how to cope with dementia by watching expert practitioners at work but I now had an Admiral Nurse. When I had written my summary of Bet's behaviour for A and the psychiatric team – I had sent a copy in to Cornwall Care with son-in-law Ian (who was working there at the time). That's how I met Loraine Butterworth who had recently been appointed to Cornwall to organise a new Admiral Team. Just as Macmillan or Marie Curie care for those with cancer, the Admiral nurses (set up and trained by Dementia UK) are there to help families who are coping with Dementia – and in particular they aim to offer support to the carers. What a god send! I cannot thank Loraine enough. Initially she offered so much practical advice – how and what to claim in terms of financial help; the wisdom of applying for 'Power of Attorney'; and the necessity to keep a sense of humour. Loraine was to stay close throughout the next stages – always responding quickly to my texts and phone calls. No doubt she will soon be in to see Bet and myself in Kenwyn. After almost two years I consider her a true friend.

I consider myself so lucky to have had the support I have had from everyone in the Health Service – those looking after Bet and those who have continued to treat me. Now Bet was being supported in 'Crossroads' I was to begin my own medical journey with a whole body bone scan closely followed by an MRI scan of my prostate area. These were relatively pleasant experiences, which is more than can be said for the urology 'flow tests'. I had to go down to Penzance for a couple of these. A rather utility side room with half a dozen other chaps of various ages and sizes – and large jugs of water! When you think your bladder is about to burst you signal to the ever-cheerful nurse and pop into the loo. High tec stuff this! A bucket with a funnel and a rather primitive gauge! Then out and up onto the couch for an ultrasound scan to inevitably show that the bladder isn't very empty. Yes I am having trouble peeing. I have told you this! I know! And now I have to drive back to Falmouth with a bladder that was hardly empty and having just downed at least two litres of water. Suffice to say that I now know most of the lay – bys en route! This was the start. Much worse was to follow!

Although I knew that cancer would eventually be diagnosed it did not seem to worry me. I was far more concerned that we could get an accurate diagnosis for Bet – although it was becoming increasingly obvious that even if my suspicion of Frontotemporal Dementia was correct no one would be able to tell me how the illness would progress. I could only deal with one day at a time – balancing my daily visits to see Bet with my own ever-increasing appointments at local hospitals.

Should I not have gone in to see Bet every day? I would have found it very difficult not to and our CPN (Community Psychiatric Nurse) 'A' really left the decision to me. In my mind I had to try to regain Bet's trust. How could I just accept that she now was afraid of me and perhaps would have been happier if I had not visited every day. Her diary gives mixed signals. She was usually pleased to see me and enjoyed the fact that I took her out for walks. At the same time it is obvious that my presence is disturbing. She claims to hear my voice during the nights and still has doubts about my faithfulness,

Today's been strange. I keep hearing Pete's voice but not actually seeing him. He's so powerful, but I still find the idea of the knives in the drawer and the whisper I heard beneath his breath as I hear most nights..
Bet Kaye 26th February 2014

I think someone's trying to play on my mind to convince me I am imagining things and there is no way out. I am sure Pete will still have those knives out and he's stronger than me
Bet Kaye 1st March 2014

I don't know what Pete's doing tonight – he's ruined our
life together by doing what he's been doing apparently
all our married life. Can't believe it's happened – and I
don't know how I feel about him any more. Will have
to see what tomorrow brings. Can't really live with him
any more… Lunch was interesting. Salad of course…
Bet Kaye 8th March 2014

Thankfully Bet's medical team seemed to believe me and accept that I had been a completely faithful husband and that I had never had the slightest intention of attacking Bet with my kitchen knives. But how close does one become in such situations to becoming the evil one?

I look closely at Bet's face. The sun doesn't shine into her room in the afternoon but the room is light. There isn't a wrinkle. Her face is as smooth as when I first met her and she has never used any makeup! She still uses lip balm as she has done for the past two years – but I don't think she can use that by herself now. I tend to include it in our afternoon rituals. I'm not sure if we are still following the drug routine or if it is even relevant now. Surely she can no longer hate me? I tell Bet that Dr K is coming to visit her soon and she attempts to smile.

Dr K is the psychiatrist who first came to see Bet at 'Crossroads'. Dr K is charming, petite and comes from Lithuania. She is one of the team who have been so supportive and have responded immediately whenever I have asked for help. She is also the only member of the team who has never been verbally or physically attacked by Bet. Bet liked her from the first meeting.

> *The neuro lady was lovely and suggested I had a tickle*
> *of a psychiatric drug – hope it has no side effects …*
> *Bet Kaye 6th March 2014*

"The woods are lovely, dark and deep ..."

Monday 12th October 2015

Bet is in the dining room today. She attempts her contorted smile as I cross over towards her and I am able to relax away some of the tension I always feel as I sign in the visitor's book and climb the stairs. It is as though I know, one day, it will all be different. She is now about to finish her yoghurt and I take over from today's cheerful carer who turns to the next chair where help is required. Not all the clients need help and there is certainly one table where there are now empty wine glasses and the full three-course menu will have been valued and tested. The dining room here is always immaculately laid out with cutlery, serviettes, drinking glasses and with a small vase of flowers on each table. 'Crossroads' too, always took great care to make dining a 'special' experience. To me it seems so important to maintain such high standards even though it may often appear that clients do not care. Sadly not all care homes take this view.

I wheel Bet back to her room but need to lift her upright after we negotiate a parking spot near the window. Her muscles are getting so much weaker and her frame, once so upright and strong, is slumping forward more each day now. As I give her a drink of tea I am aware of how her posture is making swallowing even more difficult. I sourced a specially shaped drinking cup on line – and that makes things so much easier. The staff here think it a great design too – but I suspect the cost may be a problem. Finances always dictate – rarely need. No that is harsh! The NHS has treated both of us so well!

Bet asks to get back into bed and carers willingly oblige. There is always such friendly banter and good humour. I don't know how these angels can do it! I admire them so much. The hoist lifts Bet's crumpled body and lowers it gently onto the bed. Two years ago she was racing me up the mountains beyond Chur and running across the Alpine meadows as though opening "The Sound of Music". Even when she first went into 'Crossroads' we would walk every day – sometimes on the beach – but usually through nearby woods. No matter how she seemed to be feeling towards me she would always let me take her out for a walk. I had quickly noted a footpath, a few hundred yards along the road, which led into a woodland area and I knew that Bet would feel happier there. Bet was to remain in 'Crossroads' for over eight weeks and we walked almost every day. Bet's limp was beginning to become more pronounced but she still had the strength and determination to stride out.

For the first few days we didn't venture out – for we were uncertain whether or not Bet would fight against returning, but as she appeared to settle we thought it worth a try. I would have my mobile with me and I knew I could phone for help if it was necessary. For the first few trips out she was still very unsure of me. She would link my arm but would steer me clear of the car park, telling me that I had a rope in the car and that she was afraid to go near it. She liked the woods, however, and that became our routine. We would talk about the woods we had known – long walks through Langdale in North Yorkshire dragging our children through miles of pine scented adventure; wooded bilberry-clad slopes in Austria where we sat on high in the mountain air and made our mouths into warrior-like grostesques. – and above all the woods of our childhoods

Bet's childhood was in Fulletby, on the edge of the Lincolnshire Wolds. Her adventures were in and around The Pot and Pan woods of Gorse Farm …

Spring was always so colourful. I remember seeing a robin's nest under a fallen tree. We peeped and saw little bright eyes watch us. This was the Top Wood, always a treasure chest with birds singing. Below the farm was a bluebell wood. In spring you could walk down there over the ant hill-studded grass to the big old fallen tree which you climbed over whilst the aroma of bluebells filled your mind. Funny how the days seemed so sunny as I roamed the fields. One year the big patch of gorse was full of linnets' nests. I had tracked all the nest and egg positions in my little book. There was a terrible storm one night which devastated the nests. Luckily the birds still had time to rebuild and lay more eggs. The circle of life goes on …
Bet's 'Childhhood Memories 2014'

A bluebell wood was an integral part of my childhood too. Out through our gate, down across two fields, and there, beyond the clear stream bubbling out from a spring, was my wood. I shared it sometimes with other children from the village, but really it belonged to me – and Lindy. Lindy was my alsation and apart from Bet I have to count her as my best friend. I think I was four or five when Lindy came into my life. I had seen her first as a small puppy, part of a litter at the home of one of my dad's pals who lived in the village. I had 'fallen in love' and my mum and dad had noted! A week or so later I was taken to an appointment at Pinderfields Hospital in Wakefield. I had developed a limp and had to see a specialist doctor. I remember clearly being asked to walk across the room with the doctor watching me and then a frightening conversation where I could understand only a smattering of what was happening – but I knew that I had to stay in hospital. I was not going home. I must have cried bitterly but I can remember that Mum promised me the puppy. They would collect it before I was to come home. I was only to stay in hospital for three days and I was to be a 'brave little man'.

Those three days turned into six months. For most of that time I was strapped onto a hideous frame where I was unable to move from my waist downwards. I suppose at that time in the late 1940's parents were not encouraged to visit their children often, and, in any case, my mum and dad were working and transport was not easy. Wakefield was a long way from home. I remember screaming for help with ungainly cumbersome 'bed pans' and feeling ignored. I gave up and fouled my bed every day and every day I would be admonished. I have vivid memories of being wheeled out onto a glass veranda and my emaciated body being invaded by wasps. Not a good time for a small boy and little wonder that I now suffer from 'white coat syndrome' with my blood pressure rising to boiling point whenever I set foot into a hospital. Eventually I was released and the limp had disappeared. At last I could meet my puppy.

I am sure that my mum and dad would have explained many times that Lindy was no longer the little puppy of my memory but the message did not dent my treasured long-held image. I sat on the carpet whilst Lindy was brought in from her kennel. I prepared my knee to hold her. The door opened and there was this huge, gigantic wolf-like creature towering above me. There was something very special between us and my fear was short-lived. We soon became almost inseparable. I think I would have slept with her in her kennel if Mum had allowed such a thing. As it was we travelled the fields together and after I started school she would come to meet me at 'home time'. I remember how strong she was – for I would cling round her shoulders and she would drag me along the grassy banks as though I was part of a rodeo show. We spent so much time together and I like to think that I became the envy of the village children who were probably terrified of my wolf. Lindy's only fault (if one can call it that) was that she would always want to go and greet other dogs – a friendly sniff and a wag of the tail! One day , I must have been eight or nine years old, she jumped over our high gate and ran across the road where a man was walking his pet. Lindy ran straight into the path of a motor cyclist who had no chance of missing her. I heard the thump and the following crash of metal on tarmac. The cyclist lay in the road motionless and Lindy crawled back to me, her back broken, and died in my arms. The motor cyclist came round and, as far as I know, suffered no lasting ill effects. From then on I would have to play alone in our woods.

I don't think the woods along from 'Crossroads' had a name – at least not one that we ever heard. They were perhaps part of the Scorrier House Estate and they adjoined the Bissoe Trail. They were deciduous and pretty bare when we first surveyed them but over the next two months we would be able to follow the birth of another natural year and it helped us, no doubt, to be more hopeful. I know when we first went there I was reminded of another of Robert Frost's poems:

Whose woods these are I think I know.
His house is in the village though;
He will not see me stopping here
To watch his woods fill up with snow...

Robert Frost

Sometimes we didn't speak , but just listened to the sounds of the woodland. I would hold Bet's hand like some tentative lover making hopeful initiatives. I was trying so hard to regain Bet's trust. I wanted to hold her and to kiss her – but I could not. There was a now a distinct barrier between us and part of me was afraid. I was not sure where we were heading but it seemed to me that we should be on that journey together. Later, when I came to read her diary entries, I realised that she had seen my efforts in a different light.

Pete came to see me and we went a nice walk ... he seems to want to take me out.
Bet Kaye 7th March 2014

Peter came to take me out for a walk. The woods are lovely now as you can see through the branches to the sky ... He tried to be romantic – well was – but he never talks of love – obviously takes it for granted ...
Bet Kaye 9th March 2014

Oh dear! How I now squirm! A fault! Why did I not tell her then, over and over again, that I loved her so much. I tell her now, every day that I visit, that I love her. If only I had realised the extent to which her paranoia was distorting our relationship, then perhaps I could have helped alleviate some of her suffering. I sensed the stress Bet was feeling and knew that she still had much anxiety about me. But only when I read her diary did I come to appreciate the extent of her fears.

I woke in the night and cried what tears I could. I am not sure if what Ann said about the divorce is true...

I am not sure what to make of it. There is no one else in my sights yet...
Bet Kaye 15th March 2014

How nice it would be to wake up with someone in my bed. I think, as Ann said, he had signed divorce papers...
Bet Kaye 17th March 2014

Very disturbed night. I kept hearing Pete. I know it was him. L said it wasn't but I've known that voice since the early 60's at The Parade, and never doubted his love or faithfulness to me. Mine has never wavered except that I keep wondering why I was brought here a whole month ago. L popped in twice and asked if I was OK. No funny business went on... I texted Pete to see if he is diverting texts which is an illegal activity. I though I could trust him but I don't know if I can...
Bet Kaye 21st March 2014

I heard Pete tonight. He's haunting me. He never lets anyone take me out unless he knows that my phone has no money on. Pete rang too and then went. Texts are being diverted left right and centre...
Bet Kaye 31st March 2014

'Texting' was to become quite a problem for us all during Bet's couple of months at 'Crossroads'. Initially Sam and other friends would receive texts which asked, or demanded, that Bet needed collecting and taken 'home'. 'Home' would not be Arwenack Avenue, for that was where the knives were – but would be some other place which in Bet's mind was safe and secure. As Bet became to know the people at Scorrier and to trust them her 'texts' took on a more disturbing tone. I would receive quite venomous messages, especially during the night, which accused me of spying and of being 'downstairs' and taking on a threatening and menacing persona. The idea that I was in control of her phone and that I was 'diverting her messages' seemed to have become the latest obsession. On my visits she would complain that there was a fault with her phone and she became angry and frustrated with it. Maybe she was finding the actually control difficult now that her fingers were perhaps not able to cope with finer movements? Or was it just that her 'reality' was seeing me still as a threat? I bought her a new phone with large buttons but even that seemed not to be sending the messages she intended. I could do nothing that was right.

Putting our house in Arwenack Avenue 'on the market' was a move that was to cause Bet so much anxiety. It didn't happen in the way I intended. I had planned a gentle period of calm where, on Bet's return home, we would discuss the future together and conclude that we needed to move. We had lived there for less than three years and it was in an ideal location – just minutes walk down to Events Square and the town centre. But it was high above the Avenue – with about ten steps up from the gate and a further flight up to the front door. I knew that when Bet was able to return home that she would find the steps difficult, and eventually impossible. I knew that she would be heart-broken to have to leave her garden and her little greenhouse – and all the raised beds I had now constructed. Last summer we had planted roses – the old-fashioned scented varieties and I knew moving away from here would be so hard. I was now having to make decisions for us both – and, for the first time, without Bet's 'oh so sensible' input. I would take things steadily – or so I planned.

I invited our friendly estate agent John Lay to call and place a valuation. This he did and I prepared him to discretely market the property at some future date. There were a few external painting jobs which needed completing and, as I hadn't the time' I approached our friend Shaun to see if he would like a bit of extra work. Shaun asked me if I would let him know if and when I decided to sell, as his mother in law would be interested. There seemed no hurry as she wasn't due to visit Falmouth until Easter which was several weeks away. I agreed that she should come round then and the family could then decide if they wanted to take things further. My plans were soon disturbed however, when, later that evening, Shaun knocked on the door and explained that his mother in law was so excited about the prospect that she was coming down from Bristol the following day. She did and she loved the house but there was no hurry she assured me, as she had a house to sell first and that could take several months. I still would have the chance to break the news gently to Bet. No! On the Monday morning plans had changed and my prospective buyer had decided to go ahead with a 'buy to let' mortgage and I was plunged headlong into agreeing a sale.

Later that day I broke the news to Bet. She was angry and there were tears. I tried to explain but whenever Bet's physical problems were mentioned then there was the usual denial and accusations – followed by the fact that all would be sorted by a visit to a chiropractor.

Pete's not really discussed the house sale and I am not happy. It is half mine so why do we need to sell it?
Bet Kaye 4th April 2014

I am sore about selling the house. I WAS NOT PROPERLY CONSULTED and I do not want to move. Pete apparently has cancer – but it was so much easier there for I could escape into the garden and seek solace. I feel trapped by that situation…
Bet Kaye 6th April 2014

I still feel sore about the house sale. Still if I get worse! Ha! I think Pete may! It's not my fault though… We had a bit of a ding dong about my leg – it could get worse!!! I need a chiropractor and acupuncture … It is really lovely to be home. I must get back as quickly as possible. The garden needs me as well as Pete…
Bet Kaye 10th April 2014

This was obviously one of the nights which Bet had spent at home. Over the previous month there had been a series of home visits. Initially E (one of the CPN's who looked after us) would bring Bet home for a few hours. We would have lunch together and gradually Bet became less tense about being in the house and the idea of 'the knives' seemed to diminish. About once a week Bet was spending a night at home. She was now willing to travel in my car and no longer seemed to be afraid of me. There were still 'voices' which caused her distress. – usually mine. Whilst on a visit home she writes that she heard L's voice out on the Avenue during the night. L was a care worker at 'Crossroads' and her diary makes much reference to him. He worked at night usually and as Bet liked to stay up late she seemed to enjoy many conversations with him. She would tell me about his family and particularly about his little girl. I remember one particular text arriving on my phone at 1am. "I am just retiring to bed. I will be making love to L!!" If only he knew!

I came to dread the nightly texts. I would no longer take my phone to bed with me but would entertain myself over breakfast. One morning, following one of Bet's visits home, I copied down this sequence:

4.02   *Wide awake now. Just going to make love to L the Apothocary!!! Love you lots. Are you awake?*

8.23   *Hello there, hope you slept well at home. The bed didn't look as though it had been slept in. Take care. Keep hearing your voice. Very distinctive.*

9.08   *I've just heard you again now. I'm just about to have my bath. I MUST BE DIRTY. CHANCE WOULD BE A FINE THING!! Xx*

As I looked up the trees were coming into leaf and
shining into the blue sky. I could hear the woods
themselves – and an insistent happy bird. This gave
me the germ of an idea for my next Jed story … and
then an afternoon of dancing and singing which I so
enjoyed…
Bet Kaye 14th April 2014

I think the woods had been good for us both.

The woods are lovely, dark and deep.
But I have promises to keep,
And miles to go before I sleep,
And miles to go before I sleep.
Robert Frost "Stopping By Woods on a Snowy evening"

9.24   Now my mirrors actually gone. Used it here at 7.30.
        If you're here please come and check.
        Bet Kaye. Mobile phone texts.

A few days later I noted down a further text which
illustrates the turmoil within Bet's mind:

18.00   Did you sleep well? I hope you did – hope you're at
        home enjoying a good meal. I do NOT go out with
        anyone here. THERE CAN BE NO SUCH relations
        conducted here without the SAY SO here from the
        management – whoever THEY, HE or SHE may be.
        Nightnight! Sleep tight. By the way I never go out
        with anyone without you ALLOWING ME TO do
        I? xxx
        Bet Kaye. Mobile phone text.

It was about this time that I tried to write down my
feelings. I wrote down as clearly and concisely as I
could my reasons for wanting to sell the house and I
left them with Bet at 'Crossroads'– hopefully for her
to read over again and perhaps, hopefully, come to
understand.

Pete presented me with a letter as to why WE needed
to sell OUR house! I feel hopelessly let down …
Bet Kaye 12th April 2014

The following day I found the letter torn into shreds
in the waste paper basket.

I can, of course, understand Bet's anger, confusion and frustration over the selling of our house – just as I can sympathise with her distrust over the 'Power of Attorney'. She did fully understand the implications although at times it became so easy to discard the fact that she was a very intelligent person. Some aspects of her 'illness' were so divergent, so perplexing and illogical. It would have been so much easier if we were just to condemn her as 'mad'. What was happening seemed far more complex, far more difficult to manage and impossible to comprehend. Had Bet lost all capacity to reason then it would have been so much easier for me to deal with. As it was, I am left with guilt.

During the two months that Bet was to spend in 'Crossroads' I was step by step being diagnosed with 'locally advanced prostate cancer'. Strangely I had no fear. The summons to the 'Nuclear Medicine Department' for a 'whole body bone scan' seemed an almost pleasant escape from my new world. A few days later and I was relaxing under space age technology for an MRI Pelvis Prostate examination and being complimented on how still and calm I had appeared. Even the biopsies didn't cause me any anxiety – although the sensation of a staple gun being fired rapidly up my bottom could hardly be described as pleasurable. The team were preparing me for the news that my prostate problem was 'serious' and were offering all kinds of support but I calmly asked that they telephone through the results. I knew that confirmation would be as it would be.

Nothing I could now do would alter the fact that I had cancer. I just hoped that I would live long enough to care for Bet for whatever time that might take. Luckily my hospital appointments and my daily visits to see Bet were both in the same direction and I would call into 'Crossroads' following the excitement of whatever I had experienced – and that is how I regarded everything. Throughout the days of treatment that were to follow I set out to observe and to learn. I was determined to make the most of whatever was to happen. I think I have always tried to find positives in whatever life could throw – and this was all to test me to the full! The NHS staff were always so cheerful and supportive. They usually knew that Bet was not well and talking to them was always of comfort. It was when I reached Bet that my heart would begin to ache. Although I would tell her about my treatment and explain the seriousness of the findings Bet would show no sympathy. My problems seemed to mean nothing to her. That was the hardest part for me to understand and to cope with.

Eight weeks after her 'admission' to 'Crossroads' Bet felt that she wanted to return home. She had spent several single nights back in our home and now felt more secure. The threat of the 'knives' seemed to have passed. The 'tickle' of medication seemed to be having the desired effect and Bet would hold my hand, as we took our daily walk through the woods, in a way that reassured me that all could be well.

9.24   *Now my mirrors actually gone. Used it here at 7.30.*
       If you're here please come and check.
       Bet Kaye. Mobile phone texts.

A few days later I noted down a further text which illustrates the turmoil within Bet's mind:

18.00   *Did you sleep well? I hope you did – hope you're at*
         home enjoying a good meal. I do NOT go out with
         anyone here. THERE CAN BE NO SUCH relations
         conducted here without the SAY SO here from the
         management – whoever THEY, HE or SHE may be.
         Nightnight! Sleep tight. By the way I never go out
         with anyone without you ALLOWING ME TO do
         I? xxx
         Bet Kaye. Mobile phone text.

It was about this time that I tried to write down my feelings. I wrote down as clearly and concisely as I could my reasons for wanting to sell the house and I left them with Bet at 'Crossroads'– hopefully for her to read over again and perhaps, hopefully, come to understand.

> *Pete presented me with a letter as to why WE needed*
> *to sell OUR house! I feel hopelessly let down …*
> *Bet Kaye 12th April 2014*

The following day I found the letter torn into shreds in the waste paper basket.

I can, of course, understand Bet's anger, confusion and frustration over the selling of our house – just as I can sympathise with her distrust over the 'Power of Attorney'. She did fully understand the implications although at times it became so easy to discard the fact that she was a very intelligent person. Some aspects of her 'illness' were so divergent, so perplexing and illogical. It would have been so much easier if we were just to condemn her as 'mad'. What was happening seemed far more complex, far more difficult to manage and impossible to comprehend. Had Bet lost all capacity to reason then it would have been so much easier for me to deal with. As it was, I am left with guilt.

During the two months that Bet was to spend in 'Crossroads' I was step by step being diagnosed with 'locally advanced prostate cancer'. Strangely I had no fear. The summons to the 'Nuclear Medicine Department' for a 'whole body bone scan' seemed an almost pleasant escape from my new world. A few days later and I was relaxing under space age technology for an MRI Pelvis Prostate examination and being complimented on how still and calm I had appeared. Even the biopsies didn't cause me any anxiety – although the sensation of a staple gun being fired rapidly up my bottom could hardly be described as pleasurable. The team were preparing me for the news that my prostate problem was 'serious' and were offering all kinds of support but I calmly asked that they telephone through the results. I knew that confirmation would be as it would be.

Nothing I could now do would alter the fact that I had cancer. I just hoped that I would live long enough to care for Bet for whatever time that might take. Luckily my hospital appointments and my daily visits to see Bet were both in the same direction and I would call into 'Crossroads' following the excitement of whatever I had experienced – and that is how I regarded everything. Throughout the days of treatment that were to follow I set out to observe and to learn. I was determined to make the most of whatever was to happen. I think I have always tried to find positives in whatever life could throw – and this was all to test me to the full! The NHS staff were always so cheerful and supportive. They usually knew that Bet was not well and talking to them was always of comfort. It was when I reached Bet that my heart would begin to ache. Although I would tell her about my treatment and explain the seriousness of the findings Bet would show no sympathy. My problems seemed to mean nothing to her. That was the hardest part for me to understand and to cope with.

Eight weeks after her 'admission' to 'Crossroads' Bet felt that she wanted to return home. She had spent several single nights back in our home and now felt more secure. The threat of the 'knives' seemed to have passed. The 'tickle' of medication seemed to be having the desired effect and Bet would hold my hand, as we took our daily walk through the woods, in a way that reassured me that all could be well.

As I looked up the trees were coming into leaf and shining into the blue sky. I could hear the woods themselves – and an insistent happy bird. This gave me the germ of an idea for my next Jed story ... and then an afternoon of dancing and singing which I so enjoyed...

Bet Kaye 14th April 2014

I think the woods had been good for us both.

The woods are lovely, dark and deep.
But I have promises to keep,
And miles to go before I sleep,
And miles to go before I sleep.
Robert Frost "Stopping By Woods on a Snowy evening"